Is Getting Rich Myth or Plan?

Vishal Uppal

Published by Kinetic Digital Publishers

www.kineticdigitalpublishers.com

For permissions, inquiries, or other correspondence, please visit our website.

Dedicated to my father,

My mentor, My guardian Angel

TABLE OF CONTENTS

Chapter 1: The Mindset of Wealth

Before you can build wealth, you must understand it. Becoming rich starts with the way you think. Wealth is as much about mental discipline as it is about financial strategy. In today's world—driven by innovation and connectivity—it rewards those who cultivate the right mindset. The wealthiest individuals leverage not only their skills but also their adaptability to economic changes and emerging trends. They recognize that wealth is not just about money but also about knowledge, connections, and the ability to seize opportunities when they arise.

To achieve long-term wealth, it is important to develop habits that support growth. This includes setting clear financial goals, adopting disciplined spending habits, and continuously expanding one's financial literacy. A strong foundation in money management enables individuals to make informed decisions and capitalize on opportunities for wealth accumulation.

1.1 Define Your "Rich"

Wealth is a deeply personal concept. For some, it's a bank balance that ensures financial security. For others, it's the freedom to pursue their passion, travel the world, or provide for their families. Begin your journey by clearly defining what being rich means to you. Is it about stability, freedom, or impact?

Understanding this definition will help you set clear goals and avoid financial decisions that don't align with your vision. It's also important to recognize that wealth is not static—your perspective may evolve as your circumstances and aspirations change.

Being rich is not solely about accumulating money. It also involves the ability to enjoy life on your own terms—whether that means having enough savings to retire early, investing in meaningful experiences, or using wealth as a tool to help others. The clearer your vision, the easier it becomes to develop strategies that align with your personal values.

Action Step: Reflect on Your Definition of Wealth

- "I want to own a home and have $1 million in investments by age 45."
- "I want to create a business that allows me to work remotely and spend more time with my family."
- "I want to retire early and dedicate my time to philanthropic efforts."

Conclusion:

Your personal definition of wealth will shape your goals and the strategies you pursue. Revisit it periodically to ensure it aligns with your evolving priorities and aspirations. Adjust your financial plan as needed to stay on track with your long-term vision.

1.2 Develop a Growth-Oriented Mindset

A growth mindset is essential for building wealth. It's the belief that abilities can be developed through dedication and hard work. This mindset fosters resilience in the face of setbacks and encourages a willingness to learn from failure—both of which are critical for financial success. Those with a growth mindset view challenges as opportunities rather than obstacles. They embrace change, consistently seek knowledge, and take action even in the face of uncertainty.

Modern Application

Personal development is a lifelong journey that not only enhances your professional abilities but also strengthens your mindset, confidence, and decision-making skills.

Expand your knowledge by exploring a variety of subjects, including finance, leadership, communication, and entrepreneurship. Books offer valuable insights from experienced individuals, allowing you to learn from their successes and mistakes. Workshops and networking events help you connect with like-minded individuals, exchange ideas, and gain new perspectives. Online courses provide flexibility, enabling you to upskill at your own pace and stay ahead in an ever-evolving job market.

Invest in personal development. Read books, attend workshops, or take online courses to continuously enhance your skills.

Seek out mentors or coaches who can guide you on your journey. Learning from those who have achieved what you aspire to can accelerate your progress and help you avoid common pitfalls. Surround yourself with individuals who challenge and inspire you, as your environment plays a significant role in shaping your growth.

In addition to knowledge, personal development also involves self-discipline, emotional intelligence, and resilience. Cultivate habits such as setting clear goals, maintaining a growth mindset, and practicing self-reflection. Engage in activities like meditation, journaling, or fitness routines that support your mental and physical well-being, as a healthy mind and body are essential for overall success.

By consistently investing in yourself, you'll be better equipped to navigate challenges, seize new opportunities, and achieve long-term financial and personal fulfilment.

Surround yourself with ambitious, growth-minded individuals who challenge and inspire you. The people you associate with can significantly influence your mindset, habits, and overall success. Being in the company of those who are driven, goal-oriented, and constantly striving for improvement can push you to set higher standards for yourself and take decisive action toward your goals.

Seek out mentors, business leaders, and peers who have achieved success in their respective fields. Engage in networking events, masterminds, and online communities where ideas and experiences are exchanged. Participate in discussions that challenge your thinking, expose you to new opportunities, and encourage you to step out of your comfort zone.

Additionally, be mindful of the energy and attitudes of those around you. Avoid spending too much time with individuals who discourage ambition, foster negativity, or operate from a scarcity mindset. Instead, cultivate relationships with people who offer constructive feedback, celebrate your progress, and support you during challenges.

Surrounding yourself with the right individuals doesn't just elevate your motivation—it also expands your knowledge, resources, and potential opportunities. As you grow, remember to offer the same value to others by sharing your insights and supporting their journeys toward success.

Develop adaptability by staying informed about industry trends, investment opportunities, and financial literacy.

The ability to pivot and make informed decisions in an ever-changing economic landscape is crucial for sustained financial growth. By keeping up with industry trends, you can identify emerging markets, disruptive innovations, and potential risks before they become widespread concerns.

Regularly consume reliable financial news from reputable websites, podcasts, and publications that provide insights into global economic movements, market fluctuations, and investment strategies. Attend conferences, webinars, and networking events to gain firsthand knowledge from experts and thought leaders in finance and business.

Expand your financial literacy by continuously educating yourself on topics such as asset diversification, tax optimization, passive income streams, and risk management. Reading books by renowned financial experts, taking online courses, and following successful investors can provide valuable strategies to enhance your financial decision-making skills.

Adaptability also involves embracing new technologies and financial tools. Understanding how digital currencies, blockchain, artificial intelligence, and automation impact industries can give you a competitive edge. Keeping an open mind to these advancements allows you to capitalize on opportunities that others might overlook.

Lastly, practice critical thinking and flexibility in financial planning. The economy and investment landscapes are dynamic, and being adaptable ensures that you can adjust your strategies as needed. Set periodic reviews for your financial plans and make data-driven adjustments to stay aligned with your long-term wealth-building goals.

Cultivate problem-solving skills and an entrepreneurial mindset to identify and capitalize on financial opportunities.

The ability to analyze challenges, develop creative solutions, and take calculated risks is essential for financial growth. Entrepreneurs and successful investors constantly assess problems and seek innovative ways to turn them into profitable ventures.

Develop your problem-solving skills by engaging in activities that require critical thinking, such as strategic games, case studies, and real-world financial scenarios. Practice breaking down complex issues into smaller, manageable parts and brainstorming multiple solutions. Learning from successful entrepreneurs and industry leaders can also provide valuable insights into effective problem-solving techniques and strategic decision-making.

An entrepreneurial mindset involves recognizing opportunities where others see obstacles. It requires a proactive approach to learning, adaptability, and resilience. Stay curious and open to new ideas by networking with forward-thinking individuals, attending industry events, and exploring emerging market trends. Keep a journal of business and investment ideas, and assess their feasibility by conducting thorough research and testing small-scale implementations before making significant commitments.

Additionally, embrace failure as part of the learning process. Every setback presents a valuable opportunity to refine your strategies and improve future decision-making. By fostering resilience and maintaining a growth-oriented perspective, you can navigate uncertainties with confidence and turn challenges into opportunities for financial success.

By continuously honing your problem-solving skills and nurturing an entrepreneurial mindset, you position yourself to seize financial opportunities, adapt to changing economic landscapes, and build long-term wealth. Cultivate a habit of curiosity—always seek new ways to improve and diversify your income streams.

A mindset of curiosity fuels innovation, creativity, and financial growth. By staying open to new ideas, industries, and technological advancements, you can identify lucrative opportunities that others may overlook.

Develop a habit of learning by actively researching different income-generating avenues, including stock market investments, real estate, digital assets, entrepreneurship, and passive income streams.

Follow industry experts, read books, listen to finance and business podcasts, and participate in workshops or mastermind groups that expose you to fresh perspectives.

Experiment with small-scale projects to test new income streams without significant financial risk. For example, consider launching a side hustle, investing in dividend-paying stocks, or monetizing a hobby through digital platforms. Each endeavour provides valuable insights into what aligns best with your skills, interests, and long-term goals.

Leverage technology to explore online business opportunities such as e-commerce, affiliate marketing, content creation, or app development. The internet has opened the door to numerous scalable income sources that often require minimal upfront investment.

Networking is also essential for discovering financial opportunities. Engage with industry professionals, entrepreneurs, and thought leaders who can offer guidance, insights, and potential collaboration. Surrounding yourself with ambitious individuals fosters inspiration and motivation to pursue financial growth.

Finally, embrace adaptability and flexibility. Economic landscapes change, and the ability to pivot and explore new revenue sources is key to maintaining financial resilience. By cultivating curiosity and adopting a proactive mindset, you can continuously expand your income streams and secure long-term financial stability.

1.3 Overcome the Fear of Wealth

Fear is a major barrier to wealth creation. Fear of failure, fear of success, and fear of change can all prevent you from pursuing opportunities. These fears often stem from past experiences, societal conditioning, or self-doubt. Many people hesitate to take financial risks because they fear losing money, making mistakes, or stepping into the unknown.

However, it's important to understand that setbacks are an inevitable part of the wealth-building journey. Those who achieve financial success do so by facing challenges head-on, learning from their experiences, and making strategic adjustments along the way.

Challenge these fears by reprogramming your thoughts and adopting a positive outlook. Recognize that financial growth requires taking calculated risks and that learning from setbacks is part of the process. Rather than allowing fear to dictate your actions, use it as a tool to develop strategic thinking and risk assessment skills.

Educate yourself about investments, entrepreneurship, and financial management to build confidence in your decisions. Wealth is often built through a series of well-informed choices, persistence, and continuous adaptation to changing market conditions. Those who attain financial prosperity don't avoid risk—they learn to manage it effectively.

Surround yourself with mentors, successful individuals, and educational resources that reinforce a success-oriented mindset. Exposure to positive influences can help diminish fear and replace it with confidence and empowerment.

Many people hold subconscious beliefs that hinder their ability to attain financial success. Negative associations with money—such as viewing it as a source of greed or corruption—can create internal resistance. These beliefs are often inherited from cultural, familial, or societal narratives.

Challenging these limiting beliefs is a crucial step toward embracing financial growth. It's essential to shift from a scarcity mindset—where money is seen as limited and unattainable—to an abundance mindset, which recognizes that wealth is achievable through effort, knowledge, and strategic planning.

To overcome financial fears and limiting beliefs, engage in activities that foster self-improvement. Read books on financial literacy, attend wealth-building seminars, or seek guidance from financial advisors. Develop a solid understanding of how money works, how investments grow, and how financial systems operate. The more knowledge you gain, the less intimidating financial decisions become.

Additionally, practicing financial affirmations and visualizing success can help rewire your subconscious mind. Affirming statements reinforce positive beliefs about money and your ability to build wealth.

Examples:

"I am capable of managing my finances wisely."

"I attract wealth and prosperity through my efforts."

Action Step: Identify and Confront Limiting Beliefs

Limiting belief	Empowering belief
• Money is the root of all evil.	• Money is a tool to create positive impact and opportunities.
• I'm not good with numbers.	• I can learn the skills needed to manage my finances effectively.
• Wealth is only for the lucky.	• Wealth is built through knowledge, effort, and strategic decision-making.
• I don't deserve wealth.	• I am capable and deserving of financial success.
• Rich people are selfish.	• Wealth allows me to help others and contribute positively to society.
• Investing is too risky.	• Smart investments, when researched properly, can lead to financial growth and security.

Conclusion:

Overcoming fear and transforming your beliefs about money takes time and effort. However, with persistence and a proactive mindset, you can break through barriers and build the financial future you envision.

1.4 Start Where You Are

You don't need to be rich to start building wealth. Begin with what you have and commit to steady growth. Small, consistent efforts compound over time into significant results. The key is to focus on progress, not perfection. Wealth-building is a marathon, not a sprint, and developing good financial habits early will lead to long-term prosperity.

It's essential to recognize that every financial decision—no matter how small—contributes to your long-term wealth. Start by understanding your current financial situation, setting small, achievable goals, and making incremental improvements. Prioritize creating an emergency fund, and gradually increase your investments over time.

Start investing with fractional shares or robo-advisors, which allow you to enter the market with minimal capital.

Investing can seem daunting, especially for beginners who may feel they need substantial funds to get started. However, modern financial tools have made it easier than ever to begin building wealth with small, manageable amounts.

Fractional shares enable investors to purchase a portion of a stock rather than a full share, making it possible to invest in high-priced stocks like Amazon or Tesla without needing thousands of dollars upfront. This strategy allows for greater portfolio diversification, reducing risk while maintaining exposure to high-quality investments.

Robo-advisors offer an automated way to invest by using algorithms to manage your portfolio based on your financial goals and risk tolerance. These platforms are ideal for beginners or those who prefer a hands-off approach to investing. They typically charge lower fees than traditional financial advisors and ensure that your portfolio remains well-balanced, with periodic rebalancing to optimize growth.

In addition to fractional shares and robo-advisors, consider exploring exchange-traded funds (ETFs), which provide diversification by allowing you to invest in multiple assets within a single fund. ETFs often track indexes, industries, or sectors, making them a cost-effective and efficient way to gain broad market exposure.

To maximize your investment strategy, start by setting clear financial goals. Determine your risk tolerance and research various investment platforms to find one that aligns with your needs. Automate contributions to your investment accounts to ensure consistent, long-term growth.

By leveraging modern investment tools and strategies, you can gradually build wealth without needing large sums of money upfront—making financial independence more accessible to everyone.

Additionally, automate your savings to build an emergency fund and ensure consistency in wealth accumulation.

Setting up automatic transfers to a dedicated savings account eliminates the temptation to spend and makes saving a consistent habit. This method allows you to grow your financial cushion steadily, without needing to manually deposit funds each month.

An emergency fund acts as a financial safety net, covering unexpected expenses such as medical bills, car repairs, or job loss. Experts recommend saving at least three to six months' worth of living expenses in an easily accessible account. Automating contributions ensures you consistently work toward this goal without the risk of forgetting or deprioritizing it.

In addition to traditional savings accounts, consider using high-yield savings accounts or money market funds to earn interest on your emergency savings. Some financial institutions also offer automatic round-up features, where purchases are rounded up to the nearest dollar and the spare change is transferred to savings.

For long-term wealth accumulation, automation can extend beyond emergency savings to include retirement accounts, investment portfolios, and other wealth-building instruments. Setting up recurring contributions to retirement funds, such as a 401(k) or IRA, ensures consistent growth while also taking advantage of employer matches and tax benefits.

By automating your savings and investments, you remove emotional decision-making and establish a disciplined approach to financial growth—making it easier to achieve long-term financial stability and build wealth.

Explore side hustles and gig economy opportunities to diversify your income streams. In today's fast-paced digital world, there are more options than ever to generate additional income outside of traditional employment. Whether you have a specialized skill, creative talent, or simply extra time, leveraging side hustles can provide financial security, flexibility, and even serve as a foundation for long-term wealth-building.

Side hustles can range from freelancing, consulting, and online businesses to passive income opportunities like blogging, affiliate marketing, and e-commerce. Platforms such as Upwork, Fiverr, and Freelancer allow individuals to monetize skills in areas like writing, graphic design, coding, and virtual assistance. For those who prefer a more hands-on approach, consider starting a local service-based business such as tutoring, pet sitting, or home organization.

The gig economy offers numerous ways to earn money on a flexible schedule. Driving for rideshare companies like Uber and Lyft, delivering food through platforms such as DoorDash or Instacart, or renting out a spare room on Airbnb can provide steady income with minimal upfront investment. Additionally, print-on-demand services, dropshipping, and digital product sales enable entrepreneurs to create scalable income streams without the need to manage inventory.

To maximize the benefits of side hustles and gig opportunities, focus on finding options that align with your interests and skills.

Start small, experiment with different avenues, and reinvest your earnings into ventures that show potential. The key to long-term success is consistency, adaptability, and a willingness to explore new opportunities as markets evolve.

Diversifying your income through side hustles not only increases financial stability but also opens doors to new professional opportunities, expanded networks, and valuable skill development. By tapping into the gig economy and entrepreneurial ventures, you can take greater control of your financial future and accelerate your path to wealth.

Track your expenses and optimize your spending to redirect funds toward long-term wealth-building.

Understanding where your money goes each month is the first step toward gaining financial control and building wealth. By closely monitoring your expenses, you can identify patterns, pinpoint wasteful spending, and make informed decisions about how to allocate your financial resources more effectively.

Start by categorizing your expenses into essentials (such as rent, utilities, and groceries) and non-essentials (such as dining out, subscriptions, and impulse purchases). Use budgeting tools and apps like Mint, YNAB (You Need a Budget), or simple spreadsheets to track your spending habits in real time. These tools offer insights into your cash flow and help highlight areas where spending can be reduced or optimized.

Once you have a clear picture of your expenses, implement strategies to minimize unnecessary costs. This may include renegotiating bills, reducing discretionary spending, or finding more cost-effective alternatives for recurring expenses.

Consider using the 50/30/20 Smart Rule:

- 50% of your income goes to needs,
- 30% to wants, and
- 20% to savings and investments.

Redirecting saved funds toward long-term wealth-building ensures your money is working for you. Invest in assets such as stocks, real estate, or retirement accounts that appreciate over time. Automating contributions to savings and investment accounts promotes consistency and discipline in your financial growth.

Additionally, consider adopting a frugal mindset by prioritizing value-based spending. This means focusing your expenditures on things that truly enhance your life while cutting back on those that do not provide long-term benefits.

Small, intentional financial adjustments can compound into significant wealth over time.

By tracking expenses, optimizing spending, and redirecting funds wisely, you establish a strong foundation for financial independence and long-term prosperity.

Develop multiple income streams, including passive income sources such as dividends, real estate, or digital assets.

Relying on a single source of income can be risky, especially in uncertain economic times. Diversifying your income not only increases financial stability but also creates opportunities for exponential wealth growth.

Passive income sources enable you to generate earnings with minimal ongoing effort. For example, investing in dividend-paying stocks provides a steady stream of income while also allowing for capital appreciation over time.

Real estate investments—such as rental properties or REITs (Real Estate Investment Trusts)—offer long-term wealth accumulation through rental income and property value appreciation.

Additionally, the rise of digital assets and online entrepreneurship has opened up new avenues for passive income. Creating and monetizing digital products such as e-books, online courses, or print-on-demand merchandise enables you to earn money without constant involvement.

Investing in cryptocurrencies, staking rewards, or decentralized finance (DeFi) projects can also be lucrative; however, these opportunities require thorough research and careful risk assessment.

Beyond passive income, consider exploring semi-passive and active income streams that align with your skills and interests. Building an online business, launching a subscription-based service, or developing intellectual property—such as patents or licensing deals—can significantly enhance your earning potential.

The key to successfully developing multiple income streams lies in strategic planning and effective time management. Start by assessing your financial goals, skill set, and available resources. Allocate your time and capital efficiently to build and sustain diverse revenue streams, ensuring each one supports your overall wealth-building strategy. By leveraging multiple income sources, you create financial resilience and unlock greater opportunities for long-term prosperity.

Set up a financial plan with both short-term and long-term goals to maintain focus and motivation. A structured financial plan provides clarity and direction, helping you make informed decisions and stay committed to your wealth-building journey.

Short-term goals typically cover a timeline of a few months to a few years and may include building an emergency fund, paying off high-interest debt, or saving for a major purchase like a car or a home down payment. These goals should be specific, measurable, and attainable to ensure steady financial progress.

Long-term goals, on the other hand, focus on wealth accumulation over several years or decades. These may include investing for retirement, achieving financial independence, purchasing real estate, or building a diversified investment portfolio. Setting clear long-term objectives helps you develop sustainable financial habits and make strategic decisions that support your financial future.

To effectively plan and track your progress, use budgeting tools, spreadsheets, or financial planning software. Break larger goals into smaller, actionable milestones and set deadlines to stay accountable. Automating your savings and investments also helps ensure consistent contributions toward both short- and long-term financial aspirations.

Review and adjust your financial plan regularly to accommodate changes in income, expenses, and market conditions. Flexibility is key, as financial landscapes evolve and personal priorities may shift over time. By staying focused on your financial goals, you create a roadmap that supports sustained wealth and long-term financial security—keeping you motivated and disciplined along the way.

By taking action today, no matter how small, you set yourself on the path toward financial independence and lasting success. Wealth is not built overnight but through deliberate and consistent effort over time. Small steps—such as setting a budget, automating your savings, or making your first investment—can lead to significant financial gains in the long run. Every decision you make today contributes to shaping your financial future.

The wealthiest individuals understand that consistency and smart decision-making are key to achieving financial freedom. They develop habits that reinforce disciplined financial practices—such as regularly reviewing their investment portfolios, seeking knowledge, and diversifying income streams. They also recognize the importance of patience and resilience, understanding that setbacks are part of the journey and can be overcome with strategic adjustments and perseverance.

Start now, learn continuously, and remain committed to your vision of wealth. The financial landscape is always evolving, and staying informed about market trends, new investment opportunities, and emerging industries will give you an advantage. Embrace lifelong learning by reading books, attending seminars, and engaging with mentors or financial advisors who can offer guidance and insight.

Conclusion:

Embrace the journey with an open mind and a willingness to grow. Financial success is not just about accumulating wealth, but also about developing a mindset of abundance, adaptability, and continuous improvement. Surround yourself with like-minded individuals who inspire and challenge you, and remain open to refining your strategies as your financial goals evolve. Every step you take today moves you closer to financial independence. By staying focused and proactive, you can build a secure and prosperous future for yourself and your loved ones.

DECIDE WHAT YOU WANT IN FUTURE

1. ______________________________

2. ______________________________

3. ______________________________

4. ______________________________

5. ______________________________

6. ______________________________

7. ______________________________

8. ______________________________

9. ______________________________

10. ______________________________

Chapter 2: Earning Beyond Limits

Your earning potential is not fixed. With the right strategies and skills, you can expand your income and create diverse streams of revenue. Let's explore actionable ways to unlock your earning potential.

2.1 Unlock Your Value

Your income is often tied to the value you bring to the marketplace. Focus on developing in-demand skills and solving problems for others.

Action Step: Conduct a self-assessment.

What skills do you have that are valuable?

Identifying your valuable skills is the first step toward unlocking your earning potential and increasing your financial opportunities. Your skills can be categorized into technical, soft, and transferable skills that can be applied across various industries and job roles.

Consider the following questions when evaluating your skill set:

Self-Discussion:

- What specialized knowledge or expertise do you possess that others find valuable?
- What technical skills do you have—such as programming, graphic design, writing, data analysis, or digital marketing?
- Do you have leadership or management experience that can be leveraged for consulting or coaching?
- Are you skilled in problem-solving and critical thinking, which can help businesses improve efficiency and operations?
- What communication skills do you have, such as public speaking, negotiation, or sales expertise?

- Are you creative and innovative in developing new ideas, content, or products?
- Do you possess financial literacy skills, such as budgeting, investing, or wealth management?
- Are you proficient in languages, making you valuable for translation, tutoring, or global business opportunities?

Ask Yourself?

- Do you have an eye for design, photography, or visual storytelling that can be monetized?
- Are you skilled in teaching, mentoring, or coaching others in a specific area?
- What problem-solving skills do you bring to the table that make you a valuable asset in any business or industry?

By identifying and refining your most valuable skills, you can position yourself for higher income potential, career advancement, and entrepreneurial success.

What problems can you solve that others are willing to pay for? (More Homework)

Understanding the problems you can solve is essential for creating value in the marketplace. People and businesses are constantly seeking solutions that make life easier, save time, or help them achieve specific goals. To uncover your potential, consider the following areas where your skills can be applied to solve real-world problems:

- **Business and Marketing Solutions:** Can you help businesses increase sales, improve branding, or optimize their digital presence?
- **Technology and Innovation:** Can you develop software, troubleshoot IT issues, or create automation systems tc streamline processes?
- **Financial Management:** Can you assist with budgeting, investment strategies, or debt management to improve financial health?

- **Education and Skill Development:** Can you teach, tutor, or coach others in areas such as language, coding, or personal development?
- **Creative Services:** Can you provide graphic design, content creation, photography, or video editing services?
- **Health and Wellness:** Can you offer fitness training, mental health support, or nutritional guidance?
- **Real Estate and Investments:** Can you advise on real estate purchases, property management, or investment opportunities?
- **Legal and Compliance Assistance:** Can you help with legal documentation, contracts, or compliance in various industries?
- **Time Management and Productivity:** Can you create strategies to help individuals or businesses improve efficiency and productivity?
- **Customer Service and Relationship Management:** Can you provide customer support solutions, client retention strategies, or sales training?

By identifying the problems you can solve, you can create a valuable service, develop a profitable business, or position yourself as an expert in your field.

What knowledge or expertise do you possess that others may find useful?

Your knowledge and expertise can be powerful assets in creating value and generating income. Everyone has unique experiences, specialized training, or practical insights that can benefit others. Consider the following areas where your knowledge may be valuable:

- **Industry-Specific Expertise:** Do you have in-depth knowledge of a particular field, such as finance, healthcare, technology, or law?
- **Technical Skills:** Are you proficient in coding, data analysis, cybersecurity, or software development?
- **Business and Marketing Acumen:** Do you understand branding, advertising strategies, or sales techniques that can help businesses grow?

- **Personal Finance and Investing:** Can you provide insights into budgeting, saving, investing, or wealth-building strategies?
- **Education and Training:** Are you skilled in teaching, mentoring, or coaching in a specific subject or skill set?
- **Health and Wellness:** Do you have knowledge about fitness, nutrition, mental health, or holistic well-being?
- **Real Estate and Property Management:** Can you offer expertise in buying, selling, or managing properties?
- **Legal and Compliance Knowledge:** Do you understand contracts, intellectual property, or industry regulations?
- **Self-Improvement and Productivity:** Have you mastered time management, goal setting, or personal development techniques?

By recognizing your unique expertise, you can leverage it to create content, offer consulting services, build digital products, or educate others. Turning your knowledge into a valuable resource can open doors to new opportunities and financial growth.

Conclusion:

Enhancing your skills through structured learning and mentorship is a strategic way to increase your value in the marketplace. Whether you're aiming to advance in your career, transition into a new industry, or strengthen your entrepreneurial capabilities, investing in continuous learning can open doors to greater opportunities.

Mentorship: Seeking mentorship accelerates learning by providing insights from experienced professionals who have already navigated your desired career path. Ways to find a mentor include:

- Connect with industry leaders through networking events and professional organizations.
- Leverage mentorship platforms like SCORE, Micro Mentor, or LinkedIn.

- Seek guidance from supervisors, professors, or experienced colleagues.
- Join mastermind groups where professionals collaborate and share strategies.
- Workshops, Webinars, and Conferences: Attending industry events provides opportunities to stay updated on trends, network with professionals, and gain insights from expert panels. Many workshops also offer hands-on training that helps you develop practical skills immediately applicable in the workplace.
- On-the-Job Training and Self-Learning: Employers often provide learning opportunities through on-the-job training, leadership programs, or specialized company-sponsored courses. Additionally, reading books, listening to podcasts, and watching educational content can complement formal learning.

By actively engaging in continuous learning through certifications, courses, and mentorship, you ensure your skills remain relevant and adaptable in a rapidly changing job market—positioning yourself for long-term success.

What industries or fields are currently in demand where your skills can be applied?

Understanding which industries are growing and in demand can help you align your skills with lucrative career opportunities. As the global economy evolves, certain sectors are experiencing rapid growth due to technological advancements, demographic shifts, and changing consumer behavior.

- **Technology & Software Development:** With increasing reliance on digital solutions, skills in programming, cybersecurity, AI, data science, and cloud computing are highly sought after.
- **Healthcare & Biotechnology:** The demand for healthcare professionals, telemedicine services, and biotech innovations continues to rise. Fields such as nursing, medical research, and pharmaceuticals remain vital.

- **Finance & Investment:** Expertise in financial planning, investment management, and fintech applications is essential as individuals and businesses seek ways to optimize and grow wealth.
- **E-Commerce & Digital Marketing:** The shift toward online shopping has created high demand for skills in SEO, content creation, social media management, and paid advertising.
- **Renewable Energy & Sustainability:** As environmental concerns grow, industries focused on solar, wind, and sustainable energy solutions need skilled professionals in engineering, operations, and project management.
- **Education & E-Learning:** Online education and corporate training continue to expand, creating opportunities for educators, course developers, and instructional designers.
- **Cybersecurity & Data Privacy:** With the rise in digital threats, organizations are investing in cybersecurity experts to safeguard sensitive information and ensure regulatory compliance.
- **Freelancing & the Gig Economy:** Platforms like Upwork and Fiverr have opened doors for independent contractors in writing, graphic design, consulting, and other flexible work arrangements.
- **Real Estate & Urban Development:** With growing urbanization, real estate professionals, property managers, and smart city planners are increasingly in demand.
- **Entertainment & Content Creation:** The creator economy—including video production, podcasting, and influencer marketing—has experienced exponential growth.

By identifying the industries where your skills align, you can position yourself for success and adapt to emerging opportunities in the job market.

2.2 Multiple Income Streams

Relying on a single source of income is risky. Building multiple income streams provides financial stability and accelerates your journey to wealth.

Modern Application:

Start a Freelance Business in Your Area of Expertise

Freelancing is an excellent way to monetize your skills, gain financial independence, and work on projects that align with your interests. By leveraging your expertise, you can create a flexible career that allows you to set your rates, choose your clients, and manage your time effectively.

Steps to Start a Successful Freelance Business (READ IT AGAIN)

- **Identify Your Niche:** Determine the specific service you will offer based on your skills and market demand. This could include graphic design, writing, programming, marketing, consulting, or other specialized expertise.
- **Build a Portfolio:** Showcase your work to attract potential clients. If you're just starting out, consider taking on a few small or personal projects to demonstrate your capabilities.
- **Create an Online Presence:** Develop a professional website or portfolio using platforms like LinkedIn, Behance, Dribbble, or a personal website to enhance your credibility.
- **Leverage Freelance Marketplaces:** Use platforms such as Upwork, Fiverr, Freelancer, and Toptal to connect with clients around the world.
- **Network and Market Your Services:** Promote your work through social media, join professional groups, and attend networking events to build relationships and gain referrals.
- **Set Competitive Pricing:** Research industry standards to set fair and sustainable rates that reflect your experience and the value you offer.
- **Manage Finances and Contracts:** Open a separate business account, use reliable invoicing tools, and document all agreements in written contracts to safeguard your interests.

- **Focus on Customer Satisfaction:** Deliver high-quality work, maintain clear communication, and foster long-term relationships to earn repeat business and positive reviews.

Starting a freelance business requires commitment and consistency. But with the right approach, it can become a sustainable, profitable venture that offers both financial and personal fulfilment.

Invest in Rental Properties or Dividend-Paying Stocks

Investing in rental properties and dividend-paying stocks can provide a reliable source of passive income while enhancing long-term financial stability. Both strategies offer unique benefits and can be tailored to suit various financial goals and risk tolerances.

Investing in Rental Properties:

- **Generate Passive Income:** Rental properties provide a consistent income stream through monthly rent payments, helping to cover mortgage costs and generate profit.
- **Appreciation Potential:** Real estate generally increases in value over time, offering capital appreciation in addition to rental income.

Tax Benefits: Property investors can take advantage of tax deductions for mortgage interest, property depreciation, and maintenance expenses.

Portfolio Diversification: Real estate adds diversity to an investment portfolio, reducing reliance on stock market performance.

Leverage Opportunities: Real estate allows investors to use borrowed capital to acquire properties, potentially maximizing returns on investment.

Long-Term Wealth Building: Owning multiple rental properties can lead to significant wealth accumulation through appreciation, rental income, and property equity.

Action Steps for Real Estate Investment:

- Research high-demand rental markets with strong job growth and stable property values.

- Calculate expected return on investment (ROI) using rental yield and cash flow analysis.
- Secure financing options, such as mortgages or real estate investment loans.
- Hire a property manager if you prefer a hands-off approach.
- Explore alternative real estate investments, such as Real Estate Investment Trusts (REITs), if direct property ownership isn't feasible.

Investing in Dividend-Paying Stocks:

- **Steady Passive Income:** Companies that offer dividends provide regular income payments, which can be reinvested for compound growth.
- **Capital Appreciation:** In addition to dividends, stocks can increase in value over time, enhancing total investment returns.
- **Low-Effort Investment:** Unlike rental properties, dividend stocks require little to no maintenance beyond regular portfolio reviews.
- **Portfolio Diversification:** Investing in dividend stocks across multiple sectors spreads risk and enhances financial resilience.
- **Compounding Effect:** Reinvesting dividends through a DRIP (Dividend Reinvestment Plan) allows for exponential growth over time.
- **Inflation Hedge:** Stocks have historically outpaced inflation, helping maintain and increase purchasing power.

Action Steps for Dividend Stock Investment:

- Research and invest in established companies with a history of consistent dividend payments.
- Look for Dividend Aristocrats and Dividend Kings—companies that have increased dividends consistently for decades.
- Diversify holdings across different industries to reduce risk.

- Monitor financial statements and payout ratios to ensure sustainable dividend payments.
- Use tax-advantaged accounts such as IRAs or 401(k)s to optimize returns and reduce tax liabilities.
- By combining rental properties and dividend-paying stocks, investors can create a balanced and diversified investment strategy that generates steady income while building long-term wealth.

The key is thorough research, careful risk assessment, and a commitment to continuous learning in both real estate and financial markets.

Create digital products, such as online courses or templates.

Digital products offer an excellent way to generate passive income while leveraging your expertise to help others. Unlike physical products, digital assets require minimal ongoing effort once created, making them a scalable and profitable business model. With the rise of e-learning and digital commerce, the demand for high-quality digital products continues to grow.

Types of Digital Products to Create:

Online Courses: Share your knowledge by creating in-depth video courses on platforms like Udemy, Teachable, or Coursera.

E-books and Guides: Write informative e-books or how-to guides that provide value in specific or niche topics.

Templates and Printables: Design customizable templates for business planners, resumes, social media content, or financial budgeting tools.

Stock Photos and Graphics: Sell high-quality photography, illustrations, or design elements for marketing and creative professionals.

Digital Planners and Journals: Create productivity tools such as goal-setting journals, habit trackers, and digital planners.

Music and Audio Content: Offer royalty-free music, sound effects, or meditation tracks for content creators and businesses.

Software and Apps: Develop SaaS products, plugins, or automation tools that address specific problems and streamline tasks for users.

Steps to Create and Sell Digital Products:

Identify Market Demand: Research trending digital products and align them with your skills and expertise.

Develop High-Quality Content: Create digital products that deliver tangible value, with well-structured content and professional design.

Choose the Right Platform: Sell on marketplaces like Etsy (for templates), Gumroad (for e-books and digital downloads), or through your own website.

Market Your Products: Use social media, SEO, and email marketing to attract and engage customers.

Automate Sales and Delivery: Set up automated systems for payment processing and product delivery to ensure a seamless customer experience.

Continuously Improve: Gather customer feedback and update your products to increase their value and attract more buyers.

By creating and selling digital products, you can build a sustainable passive income stream while reaching a global audience. With the right strategy, digital assets can become a lucrative component of your wealth-building journey.

Monetize a Blog or YouTube Channel Through Ads, Sponsorships, or Memberships.

Building a blog or YouTube channel is a powerful way to establish your personal brand, share valuable content, and generate income through multiple revenue streams. With dedication, consistency, and strategic monetization methods, content creators can transform their platforms into profitable assets.

Ways to Monetize a Blog or YouTube Channel:

Advertising Revenue:

- Enable Google AdSense on your blog or YouTube channel to earn from display ads.

- Optimize your content for higher ad engagement by focusing on relevant keywords and understanding audience preferences.

Sponsorships and Brand Partnerships:

- Collaborate with brands that align with your niche to create sponsored content.
- Negotiate paid promotions, where companies pay you to feature their products or services within your content.
- Offer affiliate marketing partnerships, earning a commission for each sale made through your referral links.

Memberships and Subscriptions:

- Utilize YouTube Memberships or Patreon to offer exclusive content, behind-the-scenes access, or premium resources to paying subscribers.
- Create a private community or newsletter where members receive unique insights, live Q&A sessions, or special training.

Selling Digital Products or Services:

- Offer e-books, online courses, templates, or exclusive guides tailored to your audience's needs.
- Provide coaching, consulting, or paid webinars for those seeking more personalized support.

Merchandising and Product Sales:

- Launch branded merchandise such as apparel, mugs, or accessories through print-on-demand services.
- Sell digital artwork, photography, or other downloadable resources that appeal to your audience.

Crowdfunding and Donations:

- Enable direct contributions through platforms like Buy Me a Coffee or Ko-fi to receive audience support.

- Use crowdfunding platforms like Kickstarter or GoFundMe for specific projects or initiatives.

Steps to Maximize Monetization:

- **Focus on High-Quality Content:** Deliver value-driven, engaging, and well-researched content that resonates with your audience.
- **Optimize for SEO and Discovery:** Implement search engine optimization (SEO) techniques, and use compelling thumbnails and titles to attract organic traffic.
- **Engage With Your Audience:** Foster a community by responding to comments, hosting live Q&A sessions, and creating interactive content.
- **Diversify Revenue Streams:** Avoid relying on a single income source by incorporating multiple monetization strategies.
- **Be Consistent and Patient:** Growing a blog or YouTube channel takes time, so remain dedicated and continually refine your content strategy.
- By implementing these monetization techniques, you can turn your blog or YouTube channel into a sustainable income source while providing value to your audience and expanding your online presence.
- Offer Consulting or Coaching Services in a Niche You Excel In.

Providing consulting or coaching services allows you to leverage your expertise and experience to help individuals or businesses achieve their goals. Whether you have skills in business strategy, personal development, health and wellness, marketing, or finance, you can transform your knowledge into a profitable service while making a meaningful impact.

Steps to Launch a Successful Consulting or Coaching Business:

Identify Your Niche:

- Determine your area of expertise and define your ideal clients.
- Focus on a specific problem you can solve effectively, such as leadership coaching, career development, financial advising, or fitness training.

Develop Your Offering:

- Clearly define your services, such as one-on-one coaching, group coaching sessions, workshops, or corporate consulting.
- Create service packages or subscription models that cater to different client needs.

Establish Credibility and Authority:

- Build a professional online presence with a website that showcases your expertise, client testimonials, and case studies.
- Share valuable content through blogs, podcasts, webinars, or free resources to position yourself as a thought leader in your niche.
- Obtain relevant certifications or accreditations to strengthen the credibility of your services.

Attract Clients:

- Utilize social media, LinkedIn, and professional networks to connect with potential clients.
- Offer free initial consultations, workshops, or webinars to demonstrate your knowledge and build trust.
- Leverage referrals and word-of-mouth marketing to grow your client base.

Set Up Systems for Efficiency:

- Use scheduling and invoicing tools like Calendly, Zoom, and Stripe to automate administrative tasks and streamline client management.
- Develop a structured coaching framework or curriculum to ensure consistency and quality in delivering results.

Scale Your Business:

- Expand by offering online courses, membership programs, or digital downloads.
- Host live events, retreats, or mastermind groups to provide higher-tier services and deepen client engagement.
- Hire additional coaches or consultants to grow your reach and impact.

Benefits of Offering Consulting or Coaching Services:

- High income potential with scalable pricing models.
- Flexibility to work remotely and set your own schedule.
- Opportunity to create a lasting impact by helping others achieve their goals.
- Ability to network and establish meaningful professional relationships.

By structuring your consulting or coaching business effectively, you can build a fulfilling and lucrative career while delivering real value to your clients.

2.3 Build Passive Income

Passive income allows you to earn money with minimal ongoing effort. By setting up systems that generate revenue automatically, you free up your time for other pursuits.

Examples:

Write an E-book and Sell It on Amazon Kindle:

Publishing an e-book is an excellent way to generate passive income while establishing authority in your niche. Amazon Kindle Direct Publishing (KDP) enables you to reach a global audience and earn royalties from digital book sales. With the right strategy, your e-book can become a sustainable source of income while providing value to readers.

Steps to Write and Sell an E-Book on Amazon Kindle:

Choose a Profitable Topic:

- Identify a subject that aligns with your expertise and provides value to readers.
- Research market demand by exploring top-selling e-books in your niche on Amazon Kindle.
- Focus on solving a specific problem or answering a common question to attract potential buyers.

Outline and Write Your E-Book:

- Structure your content with an engaging introduction, informative chapters, and a compelling conclusion.
- Use clear, concise language that resonates with your target audience.
- Edit and proofread thoroughly to ensure high-quality content.

Format Your E-Book for Kindle:

- Use Amazon's Kindle Create tool or format your book in a Kindle-friendly format such as MOBI or EPUB.
- Ensure proper font styles, spacing, and headers to deliver a professional reading experience.

Design a Professional Cover:

- Your book cover is the first thing potential buyers see, so invest in a high-quality, visually appealing design.
- Use tools like Canva, Adobe Illustrator, or hire a professional designer to create an eye-catching cover.

Publish via Amazon Kindle Direct Publishing (KDP):

- Sign up for KDP at kdp.amazon.com.
- Upload your E-book manuscript and cover.
- Set your pricing and royalty options (Amazon offers 35% and 70% royalty plans based on book pricing).

Optimize for Discoverability:

- Choose relevant keywords and categories to improve search visibility.
- Write a compelling book description that persuades readers to buy.

Promote Your E-Book:

- Use social media platforms to announce your book launch.
- Offer limited-time promotions or free book giveaways to build momentum and gather reviews.
- Run Amazon ads or leverage email marketing to drive more sales.

Leverage Multiple Income Streams:

- Convert your E-book into an audiobook to reach a wider audience.
- Repurpose your content into a course, blog series, or consulting service.

Benefits of Selling an E-Book on Kindle:

- Passive Income: Earn royalties for years with minimal ongoing effort.
- Low Startup Cost: No need for printing, shipping, or inventory.
- Global Reach: Amazon's Kindle store gives you access to readers worldwide.

Brand Authority: Establish yourself as an expert in your field.

By following these steps, you can successfully write, publish, and market an E-book on Amazon Kindle, creating a long-term revenue stream while sharing your knowledge with a global audience.

Build a Subscription-Based Service:

Creating a subscription-based service is an effective way to generate recurring revenue while consistently delivering value to your customers. Whether offering exclusive content, premium resources, or ongoing services, a well-structured subscription model can provide both financial stability and customer loyalty.

Steps to Build a Successful Subscription-Based Service:

Choose a Niche and Value Proposition:

- Identify a specific market need or problem you can solve.
- Define the unique value your subscription service will provide.
- Examples: exclusive courses, premium newsletters, business coaching, digital tools, or software-as-a-service (SaaS).

Determine Your Pricing Model:

- Offer tiered pricing to cater to different customer needs (e.g., Basic, Premium, VIP).
- Decide between monthly, quarterly, or annual subscription plans.
- Consider offering a free trial or introductory discount to attract new subscribers.

Develop High-Quality Content or Services:

- Ensure that subscribers receive exclusive, valuable, and regularly updated content.
- Create a structured release schedule to maintain engagement.
- Examples: exclusive training videos, private communities, templates, or consulting services.

Build a Community Around Your Service:

- Engage with subscribers through private groups, forums, or live Q&A sessions.
- Encourage user feedback and testimonials to continually improve your offerings.
- Provide incentives for referrals and reward long-term subscribers.

Market and Scale Your Subscription Service:

- Use social media, email marketing, and content marketing to attract new subscribers.
- Leverage paid ads and partnerships with influencers in your niche.
- Offer exclusive perks and bonuses for long-term subscribers to boost retention rates.

Benefits of a Subscription-Based Service:

- **Predictable Revenue:** Recurring payments create a stable and reliable income stream.
- **Customer Loyalty:** Ongoing value encourages long-term engagement and retention.
- **Scalability:** Easily expand your offerings as your subscriber base grows.
- **Passive Income Potential:** Automate content delivery to generate income with minimal ongoing effort.

By building a subscription-based service, you can create sustainable, scalable income while consistently providing value to your audience. A well-planned model ensures long-term growth and financial success.

Invest in REITs (Real Estate Investment Trusts):

Real Estate Investment Trusts (REITs) offer an accessible way to invest in real estate without the need to buy or manage physical properties. They provide investors with a passive income stream through dividends while also benefiting from property appreciation and overall market growth. REITs own, operate, or finance income-producing real estate across various sectors, such as commercial, residential, healthcare, and industrial properties.

Types of REITs:

- **Equity REITs:** Own and manage income-generating real estate properties, such as office buildings, shopping malls, and apartment complexes.
- **Mortgage REITs (mREITs):** Invest in mortgages and mortgage-backed securities, earning profits primarily from the interest on real estate financing.
- **Hybrid REITs:** Combine elements of both equity and mortgage REITs, offering diversified exposure to both property ownership and real estate financing.
- **Publicly Traded REITs:** Listed on stock exchanges and can be bought and sold like regular stocks.
- **Non-Traded REITs:** Not listed on public exchanges and often require longer-term investment commitments.
- **Private REITs:** Typically accessible only to accredited investors and institutions, with higher investment minimums.

Benefits of Investing in REITs:

- **Passive Income:** REITs are required to distribute at least 90% of their taxable income to shareholders in the form of dividends.
- **Diversification:** Provides exposure to real estate assets without the need for direct ownership.
- **Liquidity:** Publicly traded REITs can be easily bought and sold on stock exchanges, offering flexibility to investors.
- **Lower Entry Cost:** Allows investors to participate in the real estate market without needing substantial capital.

- **Tax Advantages:** Dividends from REITs may offer more favorable tax treatment compared to ordinary income.

How to Invest in REITs:

- **Research and Choose a REIT Type:** Select REITs based on industry focus, growth potential, and your risk tolerance.
- **Open a Brokerage Account:** Invest in publicly traded REITs through platforms like Fidelity, Charles Schwab, or E-Trade.
- **Diversify Your Holdings:** Spread investments across multiple REITs or sectors to reduce risk.
- **Monitor Performance:** Track REIT financials, occupancy rates, and broader economic trends impacting real estate markets.
- **Reinvest Dividends:** Use a dividend reinvestment plan (DRIP) to compound returns over time.

Considerations and Risks:

- **Market Fluctuations:** REITs can be affected by interest rate changes, economic downturns, and real estate market trends.
- **Management Fees:** Some REITs charge higher fees, which can reduce net returns.
- **Illiquidity in Private and Non-Traded REITs:** Limited ability to sell shares compared to publicly traded REITs.

By investing in REITs, you can build long-term wealth, earn passive income, and gain real estate exposure with flexibility and liquidity, making them a valuable addition to a diversified investment portfolio.

Create an Online Course and Sell It on Platforms Like Udemy or Teachable:

Creating an online course is an excellent way to monetize your knowledge, reach a global audience, and generate passive income. With the rise of e-learning, more people are seeking online courses to develop new skills, advance their careers, or explore personal interests. By structuring your expertise into a comprehensive course, you can establish yourself as an authority in your field while building a sustainable income stream.

Steps to Create and Sell an Online Course:

Choose a Profitable Course Topic:

- Identify a subject where you have expertise and can provide real value.
- Research market demand by analyzing top-selling courses on Udemy, Teachable, or Coursera.
- Focus on a specific problem that your course will solve for learners.

Plan and Structure Your Course:

- Outline the key learning objectives and develop a clear, step-by-step curriculum.
- Break down content into manageable modules or lessons.
- Include quizzes, assignments, and practical exercises to enhance engagement and reinforce learning.

Create High-Quality Content:

- Use clear, concise, and engaging teaching methods.
- Record professional video lectures with good lighting, clear audio, and high-quality visuals.
- Supplement video content with downloadable PDFs, worksheets, and additional resources.
- Incorporate screen recordings, animations, or live demonstrations to make learning more interactive.

Choose the Right Platform for Selling Your Course:

- **Udemy:** Ideal for reaching a large audience; offers built-in marketing support and established credibility.

- **Teachable:** Provides more control over pricing, branding, and course customization.
- Thinkific, Kajabi, and Podia: Alternative platforms for hosting and selling courses independently with greater flexibility.
- **Your Own Website:** Allows full control over pricing, branding, student engagement, and marketing strategies.

Price Your Course Strategically:

- Research competitor pricing and set a competitive yet profitable price point.
- Offer discounts, limited-time promotions, or bundled packages to attract students.
- Consider a subscription model or membership site to provide ongoing learning opportunities and continuous revenue.

Market and Promote Your Course:

- Use social media, email marketing, and content marketing to generate interest and drive traffic to your course.
- Leverage YouTube, blogs, or free webinars to showcase your expertise and build trust with potential students.
- Run targeted Facebook and Google ads to reach your ideal audience.
- Build an affiliate program where others can promote your course in exchange for a commission.

Engage with Your Students:

- Respond to student questions promptly and provide meaningful feedback on assignments.
- Create a community around your course through discussion forums or private groups.
- Offer live Q&A sessions, bonus content, or ongoing support to keep students engaged and motivated.

Benefits of Selling an Online Course:

- **Scalability:** Teach once and sell infinitely without additional effort.
- **Passive Income:** Earn money while helping others learn valuable new skills.
- **Global Reach:** Access a worldwide audience without geographical limitations.
- **Authority Building:** Position yourself as an expert in your field.

By following these steps, you can successfully create, launch, and market an online course that not only generates revenue but also empowers students with valuable knowledge.

Invest in Peer-to-Peer Lending Platforms:

Peer-to-peer (P2P) lending platforms offer an alternative investment opportunity by allowing individuals to lend money directly to borrowers, bypassing traditional financial institutions. This investment strategy enables investors to earn interest on loans while providing funding to individuals or small businesses that may not have access to traditional bank loans.

How Peer-to-Peer Lending Works:

- **Investor Role:** You act as the lender, funding loans in exchange for interest payments.
- **Borrower Profiles:** P2P platforms assess borrowers' creditworthiness and categorize them into different risk levels.
- **Diversification Options:** Investors can spread their capital across multiple loans to minimize risk.
- **Automated Investing:** Many platforms offer automated investment tools to match investors with loans that fit their risk tolerance.
- **Repayments and Returns:** Borrowers make monthly payments, which include both principal and interest, providing regular returns for investors.

Benefits of Investing in P2P Lending:

- **Higher Potential Returns:** P2P lending often provides better interest rates than traditional savings accounts or bonds.
- **Diversification:** Allows investors to distribute funds across multiple borrowers to reduce exposure to individual defaults.
- **Passive Income:** Generates consistent cash flow through regular loan repayments.
- **Accessibility:** Requires lower capital investment compared to traditional lending methods.
- **Supporting Small Businesses and Individuals:** Helps underserved borrowers access funding for personal or business needs.

Popular Peer-to-Peer Lending Platforms:

- **LendingClub:** One of the largest P2P lending platforms, offering consumer and small business loans.
- **Prosper:** Allows individuals to invest in personal loans with varying risk levels.
- **Fundrise:** Focuses on real estate crowdfunding and P2P lending opportunities.
- **Upstart:** Uses AI technology to assess creditworthiness beyond traditional FICO scores.

Risks and Considerations:

- **Default Risk:** Borrowers may default on loans, leading to potential investor losses.
- **Liquidity Concerns:** P2P loans often have fixed terms, making it difficult to withdraw invested funds early.
- **Platform Reliability:** Choosing reputable, well-established platforms is essential to avoid fraudulent operations.

- **Economic Fluctuations:** A downturn in the economy can increase borrower defaults and negatively impact returns.

How to Get Started:

- Choose a reputable P2P platform based on loan types, historical performance, and investor protection measures.
- Start with a small investment and gradually increase your exposure as you gain experience.
- Diversify across multiple loans and borrower risk levels to mitigate default risk.
- Reinvest earnings to compound returns and maximize long-term gains.
- Monitor platform performance, borrower trends, and adjust your investment strategies as needed.
- Investing in peer-to-peer lending platforms can be a valuable addition to a diversified investment portfolio, offering the potential for high returns while supporting borrowers in need of financing.
- By carefully selecting platforms and actively managing risk, investors can generate passive income and achieve steady financial growth over time.

Start an Affiliate Marketing Website That Earns Commissions on Product Sales:

Affiliate marketing is a low-cost, scalable business model that allows you to earn passive income by promoting products or services from other companies. As an affiliate marketer, you earn a commission whenever a customer makes a purchase through your referral link. This model is ideal for those who want to generate online income without the need to create their own products.

Steps to Start an Affiliate Marketing Website:

Choose a Niche:

- Focus on a topic that interests you and has strong market demand.
- Research profitable niches such as technology, health and wellness, personal finance, or lifestyle.
- Consider targeting a specific audience segment to differentiate yourself from competitors.

Set Up a Website or Blog:

- Register a domain name and choose a reliable web hosting service.
- Build your site using WordPress, Wix, or another website builder.
- Optimize your website for SEO to attract organic traffic from search engines.

Join Affiliate Programs:

- Sign up for affiliate networks such as Amazon Associates, ShareASale, CJ Affiliate, or Rakuten.
- Partner with companies that offer commission-based promotions for products aligned with your niche.
- Get unique referral links to track your sales and earnings.

Create High-Quality Content:

- Write product reviews, comparison articles, and how-to guides related to your niche.
- Include SEO-optimized keywords naturally to rank higher on search engines.
- Use engaging visuals, videos, and infographics to capture and retain readers' attention.

Drive Traffic to Your Website:

- Implement SEO strategies to increase organic reach.
- Use social media marketing, email marketing, and paid advertising to generate website visitors.
- Leverage platforms like YouTube, Pinterest, or TikTok to create complementary content that drives traffic to your site.

Optimize and Scale Your Earnings:

- Test different affiliate programs to find the most profitable partnerships.
- Build an email list to engage your audience and promote products directly.
- Expand your content strategy by adding video tutorials, case studies, and expert interviews.
- Analyze website analytics to refine your approach and increase conversions.

Benefits of Affiliate Marketing:

- **Low Startup Cost:** No need to create products or handle inventory.
- **Scalability:** Income grows as website traffic increases.
- **Passive Income:** Once set up, affiliate links continue to generate revenue with minimal ongoing effort.
- **Diverse Income Streams:** Promote multiple products across different affiliate programs.

By consistently producing valuable content and optimizing your website for conversions, you can turn affiliate marketing into a sustainable income stream, providing long-term financial rewards.

Develop an App or Software Tool That Provides Value to Users:

Creating an app or software tool is a powerful way to generate revenue while solving real-world problems for users. With the increasing reliance on technology in daily life, businesses and individuals are constantly seeking digital solutions to enhance productivity, streamline tasks, and improve user experiences. Whether you're a developer or an entrepreneur with a unique idea, launching an app or software product can lead to substantial financial success.

Steps to Develop and Monetize an App or Software Tool:

Identify a Market Need:

- Conduct market research to uncover gaps in existing apps or software solutions.
- Identify common pain points faced by businesses or individuals and design a tool to address those challenges.
- Validate your idea by gathering feedback from potential users and testing demand through surveys or beta sign-ups.

Define the Core Features and Functionality:

- Outline the primary functions that will deliver the most value to users.
- Prioritize simplicity and usability to ensure a seamless and intuitive user experience.
- Consider integrating AI, automation, or data-driven insights to enhance functionality and efficiency.
- Ensure scalability by planning for potential upgrades and future developments.

Choose the Right Development Approach:

- **No-Code/Low-Code Platforms:** Ideal for non-developers, using tools like Bubble, Adalo, or Glide to quickly build functional apps without extensive coding knowledge.

- **Custom Development:** Hire a development team or build it yourself using programming languages such as Python, Swift, Java, or Kotlin.
- **Outsource vs. In-House:** Decide whether to hire freelance developers, partner with a development agency, or manage the build internally.
- **Cloud Integration:** Utilize cloud-based services like AWS, Google Cloud, or Microsoft Azure for secure storage, scalability, and infrastructure support.

Develop a Minimum Viable Product (MVP):

- Start with a basic version that includes only the essential features.
- Test the MVP with early adopters to gather feedback and refine the product.
- Iterate based on user responses to improve performance, usability, and functionality.
- Ensure cross-platform compatibility for web, iOS, and Android users to maximize reach.

Monetization Strategies:

- **Freemium Model:** Offer basic features for free, with premium upgrades available for a fee.
- **Subscription-Based:** Charge monthly or annual fees for continued access to advanced features and support.
- **In-App Purchases:** Allow users to buy additional features, tools, or virtual goods within the app.
- **Advertising Revenue:** Earn income from ads displayed within the app interface.
- **Enterprise Licensing:** Sell software licenses to businesses for organization-wide or bulk usage.
- **Affiliate Partnerships:** Collaborate with third-party services to generate commissions through referral links or integrations.

Launch and Market Your App or Software Tool:

- Publish on major platforms such as the Apple App Store, Google Play, or relevant software marketplaces.
- Use content marketing, social media campaigns, and paid advertising to reach your target audience.
- Offer promotional discounts or early-bird pricing to attract initial users and generate momentum.
- Leverage influencer marketing, tech blogs, and PR campaigns to build credibility and awareness.
- Optimize app store listings with strategic keywords, high-quality screenshots, and compelling descriptions to improve discoverability.

Maintain and Scale Your Product:

- Regularly update the software to fix bugs, enhance security, and improve functionality.
- Gather analytics and user feedback to continuously enhance the user experience.
- Expand by adding new features, integrations, or targeting additional market segments.
- Introduce AI-driven automation or machine learning capabilities for smarter and more personalized user interactions.
- Explore strategic partnerships or acquisition opportunities to accelerate growth and broaden your reach.

Benefits of Developing an App or Software Tool:

- **Scalability:** Apps and software tools can grow rapidly when there is high demand.
- **Passive Revenue Streams:** Various monetization models can generate recurring income over time.

- **Global Reach:** A successful app can attract users worldwide with minimal operational costs.
- **Competitive Advantage:** A unique, well-designed tool can establish your brand as a leader in the industry.
- **Automation of Revenue:** Once launched, an app or software tool can function with minimal supervision, creating an ongoing source of income.
- **Long-Term Value:** Unlike physical products, digital products require lower maintenance and tend to have a longer lifespan in the market.

By leveraging technology and identifying user needs, you can create a valuable app or software product that generates income while making a meaningful impact in the digital landscape. Whether you are solving an existing problem or introducing a new, innovative solution, the key to success lies in usability, scalability, and continuous improvement.

License Your Artwork, Music, or Digital Content for Royalties:

Licensing your creative work allows you to earn passive income by granting others the right to use your intellectual property while retaining ownership. This model is ideal for artists, musicians, photographers, writers, and digital creators who want to monetize their work without selling full rights.

Steps to License Your Creative Content for Royalties:

Create High-Quality Work:

- Ensure your artwork, music, or digital content is original, high-resolution, and professionally crafted.
- Optimize your work for different formats to make it suitable for various markets and uses.

Understand Licensing Types:

- **Exclusive vs. Non-Exclusive Licensing:** Exclusive licensing grants sole usage rights to a single buyer, while non-exclusive licensing allows multiple buyers to use your content.

- **Royalty-Free vs. Rights-Managed:** Royalty-free licensing permits unlimited use after purchase, while rights-managed licensing specifies terms, usage limits, and fees.
- **Creative Commons:** Some creators offer content under Creative Commons licenses, allowing use under specific conditions while still retaining ownership.

Register Your Work for Copyright Protection:

- Secure legal ownership of your creations by registering them with the appropriate copyright office in your country.
- For music, consider registering with performance rights organizations (PROs) such as ASCAP, BMI, or SESAC to collect royalties from public performances.

Choose the Right Licensing Platform:

- **For Artwork and Photography:** Shutterstock, Adobe Stock, Getty Images, Alamy, Fine Art America.
- **For Music and Audio:** Epidemic Sound, AudioJungle, Pond5, Artlist, SoundCloud Monetization.
- **For Video Content:** Vimeo On Demand, Storyblocks, Envato Elements, Pixels.
- **For Digital Products:** Gumroad, Creative Market, Etsy (for printables, templates, and digital designs).

Set Licensing Fees and Terms:

- Determine whether you'll charge a one-time fee, recurring royalties, or use a revenue-sharing model.
- Clearly define usage rights, duration, and limitations to protect your intellectual property.
- Offer tiered pricing for different licensing needs, such as personal use versus commercial use.

Promote Your Licensed Work:

- Use social media, your website, and digital marketing strategies to showcase your portfolio.
- Collaborate with influencers, brands, or agencies seeking licensed content.
- Join online creative communities to expand your network and attract new licensing opportunities.

Monitor and Enforce Licensing Agreements:

- Use digital tracking tools to ensure compliance with licensing terms.
- Work with legal professionals to draft clear contracts and address any instances of unauthorized usage.
- Continuously update and expand your portfolio to attract more clients.

Benefits of Licensing Your Creative Work:

- **Passive Income:** Earn royalties without actively creating new content for each sale.
- **Global Reach:** Digital licensing platforms expose your work to international markets.
- **Retained Ownership:** Keep full rights while allowing others to use your work under agreed terms.
- **Scalability:** License a single piece of content to multiple buyers, maximizing your revenue potential.
- **Diverse Monetization Channels:** Sell through multiple platforms and explore different licensing models.

By licensing your artwork, music, or digital content, you can turn your creative passion into a sustainable income stream while maintaining full control over your intellectual property. Whether you're a visual artist, musician, or digital creator, this strategy enables you to monetize your work for years to come.

2.4 Scale Your Efforts

To achieve exponential growth, focus on scalability. Create systems, products, or services that can expand without requiring a proportional increase in effort or resources.

Modern Application:

Automate Repetitive Tasks in Your Business

Automation is a powerful strategy for increasing efficiency, reducing workload, and improving business scalability. By automating repetitive tasks, you can focus on high-value activities such as strategy, innovation, and customer engagement while minimizing time-consuming manual work.

Steps to Automate Repetitive Tasks in Your Business:

Identify Repetitive Processes:

- List tasks that require frequent manual input, such as invoicing, email follow-ups, social media posting, and data entry.
- Look for bottlenecks that slow down productivity and can be optimized through automation tools.

Choose the Right Automation Tools:

- **Marketing Automation:** Use platforms like HubSpot, Mailchimp, or ConvertKit for email marketing, lead nurturing, and campaign tracking.
- **Social Media Management:** Automate post scheduling and analytics tracking with tools such as Buffer, Hootsuite, or Later.
- **Accounting and Finance:** Streamline invoicing, bookkeeping, and tax calculations using QuickBooks, Xero, or FreshBooks.
- **Customer Support:** Implement chatbots and AI-driven responses with tools like Intercom, Drift, or Zendesk.

- **E-Commerce and Sales Automation:** Automate abandoned cart emails, payment reminders, and inventory tracking with Shopify, WooCommerce, or Salesforce.
- **Project Management:** Organize workflows and delegate tasks efficiently using Trello, Asana, or Monday.com.
- **HR and Payroll:** Use Gusto, ADP, or BambooHR to automate payroll, onboarding, and employee scheduling.

Integrate Business Systems:

- Use automation platforms like Zapier, Make (formerly Integromat), or Microsoft Power Automate to connect different business apps and create seamless workflows.
- Ensure data synchronization between sales, marketing, finance, and customer support teams to maximize efficiency.

Implement AI and Machine Learning:

- Utilize AI-driven analytics for sales forecasting, customer insights, and trend analysis.
- Implement AI-powered chatbots to enhance customer service and reduce response times.
- Use AI-generated content tools to create marketing materials, ad copy, and blog posts more efficiently.

Set Up Recurring Workflows:

- Automate recurring billing and subscription management for membership-based businesses.
- Schedule automated performance reports and analytics reviews to consistently track business growth.
- Enable automated appointment scheduling using tools like Calendly or Acuity Scheduling.

Monitor and Optimize Automation Systems:

- Regularly evaluate the effectiveness of your automation tools and update processes as needed.
- Gather feedback from team members and customers to ensure a seamless, user-friendly experience.
- Adjust workflows to incorporate new technologies and continuously improve efficiency over time.

Benefits of Automating Repetitive Tasks:

- **Time Efficiency:** Save hours each week by eliminating manual tasks.
- **Reduced Human Error:** Automation minimizes the risk of mistakes in data entry and calculations.
- **Cost Savings:** Reduce labor costs by automating repetitive operations with technology.
- **Scalability:** Easily manage growing workloads without the need to hire additional staff.
- **Improved Customer Experience:** Faster response times and streamlined operations enhance customer satisfaction and loyalty.

By implementing automation in your business, you can free up valuable time, increase productivity, and focus on scaling and innovation. Whether you're a solo entrepreneur or running a large business, automating repetitive tasks ensures long-term growth, operational efficiency, and a strong foundation for future success.

Partner with Others to Reach New Audiences

Collaboration is a powerful strategy for expanding your reach, gaining credibility, and increasing your income potential. By partnering with individuals, brands, or businesses that complement your expertise, you can tap into new markets and accelerate growth.

Ways to Partner with Others to Expand Your Audience:

Strategic Business Partnerships:

- Collaborate with brands or businesses in your niche to cross-promote products or services.
- Form partnerships where both parties benefit through joint webinars, live events, or co-branded marketing campaigns.

Affiliate and Referral Programs:

- Partner with influencers, bloggers, or industry leaders to promote your products in exchange for commissions.
- Create an affiliate program that allows others to earn a percentage by referring customers to your business.

Joint Content Creation:

- Co-host a podcast, blog series, or YouTube videos with experts in your field to leverage each other's audiences.
- Collaborate on research studies, white papers, or ebooks to establish greater credibility and authority in your niche.

Guest Appearances and Features:

- Write guest blog posts for established websites and publications in your industry.
- Appear as a guest on podcasts, webinars, or social media live sessions to introduce yourself to new audiences and showcase your expertise.

Social Media Collaborations:

- Run Instagram takeovers or TikTok collaborations to introduce your brand to new followers and expand your reach.
- Participate in Twitter chats, LinkedIn discussions, or Facebook groups where your expertise adds value to the conversation.

Industry Events and Networking:

- Attend conferences, workshops, and trade shows to connect with potential partners and collaborators.
- Speak at events or participate in panel discussions to increase brand awareness and establish yourself as an authority in your field.

Bundle Offers and Cross-Promotions:

- Offer bundled deals with complementary businesses, providing customers with added value through multiple products or services.
- Cross-promote each other's email lists to introduce engaged audiences to new offerings and build mutually beneficial exposure.

Benefits of Partnering with Others:

- **Increased Exposure:** Leverage the existing audiences of your partners to boost brand visibility.
- **Enhanced Credibility:** Aligning with reputable individuals or brands helps build trust with new audiences.
- **Cost-Effective Marketing:** Collaboration often reduces advertising costs while yielding higher engagement rates.
- **Access to New Markets:** Enter different industries or reach new demographics through strategic partnerships.

By working with the right partners, you can accelerate your reach, establish authority, and create mutually beneficial growth opportunities. A well-planned partnership strategy allows you to scale your business faster while maximizing your influence within your industry. Explore software or platforms that can multiply your impact.

Leveraging the right software and platforms can exponentially increase your efficiency, reach, and revenue potential. Whether you're a business owner, entrepreneur, content creator, or freelancer, using digital tools enables you to automate processes, expand your audience, and scale your operations with minimal manual effort.

Types of Software and Platforms to Multiply Your Impact:

Marketing and Social Media Automation:

- **Hootsuite, Buffer, Later:** Schedule and manage social media content across multiple platforms.
- **Canva, Adobe Creative Cloud:** Create high-quality marketing materials, graphics, and brand visuals.
- **ConvertKit, Mailchimp, ActiveCampaign:** Automate email marketing campaigns and enhance customer engagement.

E-Learning and Digital Product Platforms:

- **Teachable, Udemy, Kajabi:** Host and sell online courses to a global audience.
- **Gumroad, Sellfy, Payhip:** Sell e-books, digital downloads, and membership-based content.
- **Thinkific, Podia:** Build a branded education platform with full control over pricing, content delivery, and student experience.

E-Commerce and Payment Processing:

- **Shopify, WooCommerce, BigCommerce:** Set up an online store to sell physical or digital products.
- **Stripe, PayPal, Square:** Securely process online payments and manage financial transactions.
- **Etsy, Amazon FBA:** Reach global customers by listing products on established marketplaces with built-in traffic.

Content Creation and Monetization:

- **YouTube, Twitch, Patreon:** Monetize video content through ad revenue, memberships, sponsorships, and fan support.
- **Medium, Substack:** Publish and monetize written content through paid subscriptions and newsletter memberships.

Business and Productivity Tools:

- **Slack, Microsoft Teams, Zoom:** Streamline communication, project discussions, and collaboration for remote or hybrid teams.
- **Notion, Trello, Asana:** Organize projects, manage tasks, and optimize workflows efficiently.Automate repetitive tasks and integrate different software platforms to create seamless workflows.

Finance and Investment Platforms:

- **Robinhood, E-Trade, Fidelity:** Simplify investing in stocks, ETFs, mutual funds, and cryptocurrencies.
- **Fundrise, Crowdstreet:** Invest in real estate projects with low capital requirements and potential passive income.
- **QuickBooks, Xero, FreshBooks:** Manage small business finances, invoicing, bookkeeping, and tax preparation.

Benefits of Using Software and Platforms to Scale Impact:

- **Time Efficiency:** Automate repetitive tasks so you can focus on strategic growth and innovation.
- **Global Reach:** Expand your audience and increase sales potential across international markets.
- **Cost-Effectiveness:** Reduce overhead costs by leveraging scalable digital solutions.
- **Increased Revenue Streams:** Monetize multiple channels simultaneously to diversify and stabilize your income.

By integrating the right software and platforms into your workflow, you can optimize your time, enhance productivity, and maximize your earning potential. Investing in technology allows you to focus on what truly matters—growing your business, expanding your impact, and achieving long-term financial success.

Create a Team or Delegate Responsibilities to Free Up Your Time

Building a team and delegating responsibilities is essential for scaling your business, increasing productivity, and focusing on high-value tasks that drive growth. As an entrepreneur, freelancer, or business owner, learning to delegate effectively ensures that operations run smoothly without requiring your constant involvement.

Steps to Build a Team and Delegate Responsibilities:

Identify Key Areas for Delegation:

- List tasks that consume too much of your time but do not require your direct involvement.
- Prioritize delegating administrative work, customer support, content management, marketing activities, and repetitive processes.

Hire the Right Team Members:

- Look for skilled professionals who align with your business goals, values, and work culture.
- Choose between hiring full-time employees, freelancers, or virtual assistants based on your specific needs and budget.
- Use platforms like Upwork, Fiverr, and LinkedIn to find and vet top talent.

Define Roles and Responsibilities Clearly:

- Create detailed job descriptions outlining key responsibilities, expectations, and performance metrics.
- Establish clear accountability by setting deadlines, deliverables, and defining reporting structures.

Implement Efficient Systems for Task Management:

- Use tools like Trello, Asana, Monday.com, or ClickUp to organize workflows and delegate tasks effectively.

- Automate task assignments, reminders, and progress tracking for smoother and more streamlined operations.

Provide Training and Resources:

- Equip your team with the necessary knowledge, tools, and support to perform their roles effectively.
- Offer clear documentation, SOPs (Standard Operating Procedures), and accessible training materials to streamline onboarding and operations.

Foster Communication and Collaboration:

- Use Slack, Microsoft Teams, or Zoom for regular team meetings and real-time communication.
- Encourage open discussions, feedback, and knowledge-sharing to strengthen collaboration and team cohesion.

Monitor Performance and Provide Feedback:

- Track individual and team progress using KPIs (Key Performance Indicators) and regular performance reviews.
- Offer constructive feedback and recognize achievements to maintain motivation, engagement, and productivity.

Let Go and Trust Your Team:

- Avoid micromanaging and empower your team members to take ownership of their work and results.
- Delegate decision-making authority when appropriate to encourage leadership development and build confidence within the team.

Benefits of Building a Team and Delegating Responsibilities:

- **More Time for Growth:** Focus on business development, innovation, and strategic planning.
- **Increased Productivity:** Leverage specialized skills within your team to enhance operational efficiency.

- **Better Work-Life Balance:** Reduce stress and avoid burnout by sharing the workload effectively.
- **Scalability:** Enable your business to expand without being limited by your personal time and capacity.

By effectively building a team and delegating tasks, you create a more sustainable and scalable business model, allowing you to achieve greater success while freeing up your time for higher-impact activities.

Develop a Franchise Model if You Have a Successful Business Concept

Expanding your business through franchising is a powerful way to scale while leveraging the capital, effort, and entrepreneurial drive of franchisees. If you have a proven business model with strong brand recognition, a franchise system allows you to grow rapidly without managing each location directly.

Steps to Develop a Franchise Model:

Evaluate Your Business for Franchise Potential:

- Ensure your business is profitable, scalable, and supported by strong market demand.
- Standardize operations, branding, and customer experience to enable easy and consistent replication.

Create a Franchise Business Plan:

- Define clear franchise goals, expansion strategies, and target markets.
- Establish legal requirements, initial investment costs, franchise fees, and revenue models.

Develop a Franchise Operations Manual:

- Document detailed procedures for marketing, customer service, training, and daily operations.
- Provide clear guidelines for maintaining brand consistency and operational standards across all franchise locations.

Build a Legal Franchise Framework:

- Register your franchise in compliance with legal regulations and franchise laws in your region.
- Draft a Franchise Disclosure Document (FDD) outlining all fees, obligations, and agreements required for franchisees.
- Protect your intellectual property, trademarks, and proprietary processes to maintain brand integrity.

Set Up a Franchise Fee Structure:

- Determine initial franchise fees, ongoing royalty percentages, and required marketing contributions.
- Offer a fair and competitive investment opportunity to attract and retain qualified franchisees.

Recruit and Train Franchisees:

- Identify entrepreneurs who align with your brand values, mission, and long-term vision.
- Develop a comprehensive training program covering daily operations, marketing strategies, financial management, and customer service.
- Provide ongoing support, mentorship, and performance tracking to help franchisees succeed and maintain brand standards.

Establish Marketing and Branding Strategies:

- Maintain a consistent brand identity, voice, and customer experience across all franchise locations.
- Develop both national and local marketing plans to attract and retain customers for each franchise.
- Utilize digital marketing, social media campaigns, and PR initiatives to promote both franchise opportunities and customer engagement.

Monitor Franchise Performance and Growth:

- Implement quality control measures, regular audits, and brand compliance checks to maintain operational standards.
- Support franchisees with continuous improvements, new innovations, and operational efficiencies to drive mutual success.
- Expand strategically by entering high-demand markets and evaluating new growth opportunities based on market research and performance data.

Benefits of Developing a Franchise Model:

- **Rapid Expansion:** Scale your business faster with lower capital investment by leveraging franchisee resources.
- **Shared Risk:** Franchisees invest their own capital, significantly reducing financial risk for the franchisor.
- **Increased Brand Reach:** Establish a strong brand presence in multiple locations through dedicated local ownership.
- **Ongoing Revenue Streams:** Generate continuous income from initial franchise fees, ongoing royalties, and marketing contributions.
- **Motivated Operators:** Franchisees have a vested interest in success, often leading to higher performance and stronger customer service at individual locations.

By developing a strong franchise model, you can transform a successful business into a nationally or even globally recognized brand. With careful planning, legal compliance, strategic marketing, and ongoing support, franchising can be an effective and sustainable path to long-term wealth creation and business expansion.

Utilize Social Media and Online Advertising to Scale Your Brand Globally

Social media and online advertising are essential tools for businesses aiming to expand their reach, attract new customers, and establish a strong global presence. By leveraging digital marketing strategies, you can efficiently scale your brand and maximize profitability.

Steps to Scale Your Brand Using Social Media and Online Advertising:

Develop a Strong Social Media Presence:

- Choose the right platforms (Instagram, Facebook, LinkedIn, Twitter, TikTok) based on your target audience and brand goals.
- Create a consistent posting schedule featuring high-quality, engaging content tailored to each platform.
- Use a mix of content types, including images, videos, live streams, stories, polls, and interactive posts to keep audiences engaged.
- Engage actively with followers by responding to comments, direct messages, and questions to build strong community relationships.

Implement Targeted Advertising Campaigns:

- Utilize paid ads on platforms such as Google, Facebook, Instagram, and LinkedIn to drive traffic and boost brand awareness.
- Define your target audience precisely using demographics, interests, online behaviours, and custom audiences.
- A/B test different ad creatives, formats, and copy to optimize conversion rates and improve campaign performance.
- Use retargeting ads to re-engage visitors who have previously interacted with your website, products, or brand content.

Leverage Influencer Marketing and Partnerships:

- Collaborate with influencers or brand ambassadors to increase credibility, expand reach, and drive engagement.
- Partner with industry leaders and niche experts to tap into their established audiences.
- Implement affiliate marketing programs to encourage referrals, drive sales, and foster brand advocacy.

Optimize Content for Global Reach:

- Create multilingual content to connect authentically with diverse global audiences.
- Apply SEO strategies tailored to rank higher in international search results.
- Tailor messaging and campaigns to align with different cultural preferences, local languages, and regional market expectations.

Utilize E-Commerce and Online Sales Platforms:

- Expand your online store presence using platforms such as Shopify, Amazon, or WooCommerce.
- Offer digital products, memberships, or subscription-based services to create recurring revenue streams.
- Use email marketing automation to nurture leads, promote new offers, and boost overall conversions.

Analyze and Adjust Marketing Strategies:

- Monitor campaign performance using analytics tools like Google Analytics, Facebook Insights, and Instagram Metrics.
- Track performance metrics such as engagement rates, conversion rates, and ROI.
- Continuously evaluate key performance indicators (KPIs) to refine strategies, allocate budget effectively, and maximize ROI.

Benefits of Scaling Your Brand with Social Media and Online Advertising:

- **Global Reach:** Instantly connect with audiences worldwide.
- **Cost-Effective Marketing:** Digital ads often deliver a higher ROI than traditional advertising.
- **Data-Driven Insights:** Use real-time analytics to optimize campaigns and increase profitability.

- **Brand Authority:** A consistent online presence establishes credibility and trust.
- **Scalability:** Easily adjust advertising budgets and strategies based on business growth.

By effectively utilizing social media and online advertising, you can scale your brand globally, attract new customers, and create sustainable revenue streams. Implementing a strategic digital marketing approach will position your brand for long-term success in an increasingly competitive marketplace.

Build an Email List and Nurture It for Long-Term Customer Engagement

An email list is one of the most valuable assets for any business, allowing direct communication with your audience, increasing customer loyalty, and driving consistent sales. Unlike social media platforms, where algorithms can limit your reach, email marketing provides a reliable and personal way to engage with your audience.

Steps to Build and Nurture an Email List:

Create a High-Value Lead Magnet:

- Offer free resources like e-books, templates, exclusive reports, or webinars in exchange for email sign-ups.
- Provide discount codes, free trials, or early access to products to incentivize subscriptions.
- Use compelling calls-to-action (CTAs) across your website, blog, and social media channels.

Choose the Right Email Marketing Platform:

- Use platforms like Mailchimp, ConvertKit, ActiveCampaign, or HubSpot for effective list management.
- Automate email sequences and segment subscribers based on their interests, behaviors, and engagement levels.

Optimize Email Signup Forms:

- Place signup forms strategically on landing pages, pop-ups, and blog posts to maximize visibility.
- Minimize required fields to increase conversion rates and reduce signup friction.

Engage Subscribers with Valuable Content:

- Send regular newsletters with insights, industry trends, and actionable tips.
- Share behind-the-scenes updates, case studies, and customer success stories to build connection and trust.
- Personalize emails by using subscribers' names and tailoring content based on their preferences and past interactions.

Create Automated Email Sequences:

- **Welcome Sequence:** Send a series of emails introducing new subscribers to your brand and offerings.
- **Drip Campaigns:** Educate subscribers on your offerings over time through a series of scheduled emails.
- **Re-engagement Emails:** Reach out to inactive subscribers with special offers, surveys, or personalized content.

Promote Your Email List:

- Use social media, blog posts, and YouTube videos to drive sign-ups.
- Run paid ads targeting potential subscribers who are interested in your niche.
- Collaborate with influencers or partners to create list-building campaigns and broaden your reach.

Analyze and Optimize Performance:

- Track open rates, click-through rates (CTR), and conversions using your email platform's analytics.
- Test different subject lines, content formats, and CTAs (calls-to-action) to improve engagement rates.
- Clean your email list regularly by removing inactive subscribers to maintain high deliverability and sender reputation.

Benefits of Email List Building and Nurturing:

- **Direct Communication:** Reach your audience without relying on third-party platforms.
- **Higher Conversion Rates:** Email marketing consistently outperforms social media in terms of ROI.
- **Customer Retention:** Build trust and foster long-term relationships with subscribers.
- **Scalability:** Grow your business by maintaining an engaged, loyal customer base.

By consistently providing value and maintaining an effective email marketing strategy, you can build a strong, engaged audience that supports your business growth for years to come.

Optimize Your Business Operations for Efficiency and Cost Reduction

Maximizing efficiency and reducing costs are essential for long-term business growth and profitability. By streamlining processes, leveraging technology, and improving resource allocation, businesses can operate more effectively while increasing profit margins.

Steps to Optimize Business Operations for Efficiency and Cost Reduction:

Evaluate Current Business Processes:

- Conduct an operational audit to identify inefficiencies and bottlenecks.

- Map out workflows to pinpoint areas where automation or restructuring can improve efficiency.
- Gather feedback from employees and customers to uncover pain points in service delivery.

Leverage Automation and Technology:

- Implement automation tools for repetitive tasks such as invoicing, customer support, and social media scheduling.
- Use AI-powered analytics to track performance metrics and optimize decision-making.
- Invest in cloud-based solutions to reduce infrastructure costs and improve team collaboration.

Streamline Supply Chain and Inventory Management:

- Negotiate with suppliers for better pricing, favourable terms, and bulk discounts.
- Adopt just-in-time (JIT) inventory strategies to reduce holding costs and minimize waste.
- Use inventory management software to track stock levels, forecast demand, and prevent over-ordering.

Improve Financial Management and Cost Control:

- Regularly review expenses and identify opportunities to cut unnecessary costs.
- Consolidate vendors and service providers to secure better pricing and streamline operations.
- Implement a budget tracking system to monitor financial health and ensure spending aligns with business goals.

Enhance Workforce Productivity:

- Provide training programs to upskill employees and increase overall efficiency.

- Use project management tools to improve workflow coordination, task tracking, and team accountability.
- Encourage a results-driven culture by setting clear performance metrics and recognizing achievements.

Optimize Marketing Strategies:

- Shift to cost-effective digital marketing methods, such as organic SEO and content marketing.
- Test and refine paid advertising campaigns to maximize return on investment (ROI).
- Leverage partnerships and referral programs to acquire new customers at a lower cost.

Implement Energy and Resource Efficiency Measures:

- Reduce utility costs by optimizing energy usage in office spaces or production facilities.
- Implement remote work policies to lower operational and overhead expenses.
- Adopt sustainable practices that not only reduce costs but also enhance brand reputation.

Monitor Performance and Continuously Improve:

- Use KPIs (Key Performance Indicators) to measure efficiency gains and cost savings.
- Regularly review business processes and adapt to changing market conditions and customer needs.
- Encourage innovation and creative problem-solving to drive ongoing improvements across departments.

Benefits of Optimizing Business Operations:

- **Increased Profitability:** Lower operational costs while maintaining or improving revenue streams.

- **Greater Efficiency:** Accelerate workflows and improve resource utilization.
- **Competitive Advantage:** More agile operations allow for better customer service and stronger market positioning.
- **Scalability:** A lean, optimized business can grow more sustainably with fewer constraints.

By continuously refining operations and eliminating inefficiencies, businesses can remain agile, reduce unnecessary expenses, and enhance overall profitability, ensuring long-term financial success.

By applying these principles, you can unlock new opportunities for income growth, financial security, and long-term wealth-building.

Chapter 3: Managing Wealth Wisely

Earning money is only the first step. Managing it wisely ensures that it grows and lasts. Proper financial management is a lifelong process that involves budgeting, saving, investing, and protecting wealth from risk. By mastering these financial principles, you ensure your money works for you—not against you.

Let's explore these crucial components in detail.

3.1 Create A Budget That Works

A budget isn't about restriction—it's about empowerment. By aligning your spending with your goals, you take control of your finances. A well-structured budget ensures you live within your means while making consistent progress toward financial stability and growth.

Steps to Create an Effective Budget:

Track Your Expenses

Record all your income and expenditures over a month to identify patterns. Understanding where your money goes is the first step to effective financial management. Use a notebook, spreadsheet, or budgeting app to log every purchase, bill payment, and income source. Categorize expenses into essential and non-essential to detect trends and eliminate unnecessary financial leaks.

Tracking expenses increases your awareness of spending habits, making it easier to adjust and redirect funds toward savings and investments. Reviewing past expenditures also helps identify recurring subscriptions, impulse purchases, and areas for optimization. Many people are surprised by how much small, frequent expenses add up—motivation enough to make smarter financial choices.

Categorize Your Spending:

Break expenses into three key categories:

Needs, Wants, and Financial Goals.

A. Needs (Essentials – 50% of Income)

These are non-negotiables—expenses required for survival and stability.

- **Housing:** Rent, mortgage, utilities
- **Food:** Groceries, basic meals
- **Healthcare:** Insurance, medical bills
- **Transportation:** Car payments, gas, public transit
- **Debt Payments:** Minimum required payments

B. Wants (Lifestyle – 30% of Income)

These are non-essential but enhance quality of life.

- **Entertainment:** Streaming services, movies, concerts
- **Dining Out:** Restaurants, coffee, takeout
- **Shopping:** Clothing, gadgets, home decor
- Travel & Leisure: Vacations, hobbies, memberships

C. Financial Goals (Wealth-Building – 20% of Income)

Future-focused expenses for long-term security and growth.

- **Savings:** Emergency fund, large purchases
- **Investments:** Stocks, real estate, retirement accounts
- **Debt Repayment:** Extra payments beyond the minimum
- **Education:** Courses, certifications, skill-building

Budget Tip: Try the 50/30/20 Rule

A widely used budgeting guideline that allocates:

- 50% to Needs
- 30% to Wants
- 20% to Financial Goals

This simple structure creates a clear, balanced approach to money management—making room for responsibility, enjoyment, and future growth.

3.2 Master the Art Of Saving

Saving is the foundation of financial security. It provides a buffer for emergencies, offers peace of mind, and builds the capital needed for investments. Without a disciplined approach to saving, achieving financial independence becomes nearly impossible.

Types of Savings

1. Emergency Fund (Financial Safety Net)

Purpose: To cover unexpected financial shocks without going into debt.

How Much? At least 3–6 months' worth of living expenses (more for self-employed individuals or those with variable income).

Uses:

- Job loss or sudden income reduction
- Medical emergencies not covered by insurance
- Urgent home or car repairs
- Unexpected travel for family emergencies

Tips for Building an Emergency Fund:

- Start small (e.g., $500–$1,000) and build over time.
- Keep it in a high-yield savings account for easy access and growth.

- Automate contributions to stay consistent.

2. Short-Term Savings (Planned Expenses)

Purpose: To cover planned, non-recurring expenses without disrupting your regular budget.

How Much?: Varies based on upcoming financial goals.

Uses:

- Travel, vacations, or special events
- Home renovations or appliance upgrades
- New gadgets (phones, laptops, gaming consoles)
- Wedding expenses or milestone celebrations

Tips for Managing Short-Term Savings:

- Use a separate savings account or sinking fund for each goal.
- Calculate the target amount and set monthly contributions.
- Consider a Certificate of Deposit (CD) or short-term investment account if the goal is 1–3 years away.

3. Retirement Savings (Long-Term Wealth Building)

Purpose: To ensure financial independence after retirement.

How Much: Aim to save 15–20% of your income annually for retirement.

Options:

- **401(k) & Employer-Sponsored Plans:** Often include company matching—maximize contributions when possible.
- **IRA (Traditional/Roth):** Tax-advantaged individual retirement accounts for personal investing.
- **Pensions & Annuities:** Fixed-income sources that provide long-term security.

- **Real Estate or Passive Income Streams:** Additional options for wealth building.

✅ **Tips for Growing Retirement Savings:**

- Contribute at least enough to receive your employer's 401(k) match—don't leave free money on the table.
- Diversify across stocks, bonds, and index funds to manage risk.
- Increase contributions whenever you receive a raise or bonus.

4. Medium-Term Savings (Major Life Goals)

💡 **Purpose:** To fund significant life events that require planning but aren't immediate.

💰 **How Much?:** Based on the size of the goal (e.g., save 10–50% of the cost annually).

📌 **Uses:**

- Down payment on a house
- Starting a business
- Buying a car (without financing)
- Education expenses (advanced degrees, children's college funds)

✅ **Tips for Medium-Term Savings:**

- Use low-risk investments (e.g., bonds, mutual funds) for moderate growth.
- Consider a high-yield savings account for liquidity.
- Plan ahead to avoid relying on debt for major purchases.

5. Sinking Funds (Specialized Savings for Recurring Expenses)

💡 **Purpose:** To break large, irregular expenses into manageable contributions over time.

💰 **How Much?:** Depends on the type and frequency of expected expenses.

📌 **Examples:**

- Annual insurance premiums (auto, home, life)
- Holiday and gift funds (birthdays, Christmas, weddings)
- Car maintenance and registration
- Medical co-pays and dental care

✅ **Tips for Using Sinking Funds:**

- Open separate accounts for different savings goals if needed.
- Allocate a fixed amount from each paycheck.
- Track your spending to stay on target.

6. Investment Savings (Wealth Growth & Passive Income)

💡 **Purpose:** To grow your money faster than through traditional savings methods.

💰 **How Much?:** Varies based on your risk tolerance and financial objectives.

📌 **Options:**

- **Stocks & ETFs:** Higher risk, higher potential returns.
- **Real Estate:** Rental income and property appreciation.
- **Index Funds & Mutual Funds:** Balanced growth with lower risk.
- **Cryptocurrency & Alternative Investments:** High-risk, long-term opportunities.

✅ **Tips for Investment Savings:**

- Start early to take advantage of compound growth.
- Diversify across various asset classes.
- Only invest what you can afford to lose in high-risk assets.

Final Thoughts: A Balanced Savings Strategy

◆ **Ideal Savings Distribution (adjust based on your financial goals):**

- **Emergency Fund:** Prioritize saving 3–6 months of living expenses.
- **Short-Term & Medium-Term Savings:** Allocate for upcoming planned expenses.
- **Retirement & Investments:** Focus on long-term financial growth and security.
- **Sinking Funds:** Prepare for irregular or seasonal costs in advance.

💡 **Start small, stay consistent, and automate your savings—**

That's the key to building lasting financial security over time.

3.3 Invest Intelligently

Investing allows your money to work for you. Rather than letting your savings sit idle in low-yield accounts, investing enables your wealth to grow exponentially over time. By understanding risk management and diversification, you can make informed decisions that strengthen your financial portfolio.

Investment Strategies

A well-planned investment strategy helps grow wealth over time, reduce financial risks, and achieve long-term financial independence. Below is a breakdown of key investment strategies with modern applications.

1. Stock Market (Growth-Oriented Investing)

💡 **Purpose:** Capitalize on long-term market growth by investing in individual stocks or ETFs.

💰 **Returns:** Historically 7–10% annually on average.

◆ **Options:**

- **Individual Stocks:** Shares in companies like Apple, Tesla, or Amazon.

- **ETFs (Exchange-Traded Funds):** Bundled stocks that track indexes (e.g., S&P 500).
- **Dividend Stocks:** Companies that pay regular income to shareholders.
- **Growth Stocks:** Firms reinvesting profits for rapid expansion.

✅ **Modern Applications:**

- Use robo-advisors (e.g., Wealthfront, Betterment) for automated investing.
- Buy fractional shares of expensive stocks like Google or Amazon.
- Apply Dollar-Cost Averaging (DCA) to invest consistently and reduce timing risk.

2. Real Estate (Asset-Backed Investment)

💡 **Purpose:** Generate passive income and build wealth through property ownership and appreciation.

💰 **Returns:** Typically 8–12% annually (depending on market and location).

📌 **Options:**

- **Rental Properties:** Earn monthly income from tenants.
- **Fix-and-Flip:** Buy low, renovate, and sell for profit.
- **REITs (Real Estate Investment Trusts):** Invest in real estate portfolios without owning physical property.
- **Short-Term Rentals:** Use platforms like Airbnb or Vrbo for higher-yield opportunities.

✅ **Modern Applications:**

- Try crowdfunded platforms like Fundrise or Roofstock for entry-level investing.
- Join real estate syndications to co-invest in large-scale properties.

- Explore tokenized real estate for blockchain-based ownership options.

3. Bonds & Fixed Income (Low-Risk Stability)

💡 **Purpose:** Earn stable and reliable income with lower volatility than the stock market.

💰 **Returns:** Generally 2–6% per year depending on the bond type.

📌 **Options:**

- **Government Bonds:** U.S. Treasury bonds—safe and government-backed.
- **Municipal Bonds:** Issued by local governments—often offer tax advantages.
- **Corporate Bonds:** Higher yields, with slightly higher risk.
- **Bond ETFs & Mutual Funds:** Convenient diversification across multiple bonds.

✅ **Modern Applications:**

- Use I Bonds (Inflation-Protected Bonds) to protect against inflation and secure fixed returns.
- Implement a laddering strategy—invest in bonds with staggered maturity dates.
- Choose diversified bond ETFs like the Vanguard Total Bond Market ETF.

4. Mutual Funds & Index Funds (Diversified, Low-Cost Growth)

💡 **Purpose:** Spread risk across multiple assets while benefiting from long-term market growth.

💰 **Returns:** Average 7–10% annually (depending on fund type).

📌 **Options:**

- **Index Funds:** Track a market index like the S&P 500 with minimal fees.
- **Mutual Funds:** Actively managed funds that select diversified stocks.
- **Target-Date Funds:** Automatically adjust asset allocation as retirement approaches.

✅ **Modern Applications:**

- Start with low-cost index funds like Vanguard VTI or VOO
- Use 401(k) and IRAs for tax-advantaged fund investing
- Consider ETFs for better liquidity and lower fees compared to some mutual funds

5. Alternative Investments (High-Risk, High-Reward)

💡 **Purpose:** Explore non-traditional assets with the potential for high returns.

💰 **Returns:** Highly variable—can range from 10% to 100%+ (with high risk).

📌 **Options:**

- **Cryptocurrency:** Bitcoin, Ethereum, and altcoins for speculative growth.
- **Commodities:** Gold, silver, oil, and agricultural goods.
- **Private Equity & Venture Capital:** Invest in startups or privately held companies.
- **Collectibles & NFTs:** Rare art, sneakers, or digital assets with market value.

✅ **Modern Applications:**

- Earn passive income through crypto staking or DeFi platforms.

- Use gold ETFs as an inflation hedge.
- Invest in startups via crowdfunding platforms like AngelList or Republic.

Modern Investment Strategies & Best Practices:

✅ **Start with Low-Cost Index Funds or ETFs**

- Offer instant diversification with minimal fees.
- Ideal for beginners seeking steady, long-term growth.

✅ **Diversify Across Asset Classes**

- Don't invest everything in one category.
- ***Example allocation:*** 60% stocks, 20% bonds, 10% real estate, 10% alternatives.

✅ **Monitor & Adjust Your Portfolio Regularly**

- Rebalance annually to maintain target risk levels.
- Adapt your portfolio based on changing financial goals and market trends.

✅ **Use Tax-Advantaged Accounts**

- Maximize contributions to 401(k), IRAs, and HSAs for tax benefits.
- These accounts can significantly boost long-term returns.

✅ **Maintain a Long-Term Focus**

- Volatility is normal—avoid emotional decisions or panic selling.
- Stick to a buy-and-hold strategy for consistent growth.

Final Thoughts: Building a Smart Investment Portfolio

📌 **Beginner Strategy:**

- 80% Index Funds/ETFs (diversified, low-cost)
- 10% Bonds (stability)

- 10% Real Estate & Alternatives (growth & passive income)

📌 **Advanced Strategy:**

- 50% Stocks & ETFs (long-term appreciation)
- 20% Real Estate (income + appreciation)
- 15% Bonds & Fixed Income (low-risk foundation)
- 15% Alternative Investments (high-reward opportunities)

💡 **The key to successful investing is diversification, consistency, and smart risk management.**

3.4 Protect Your Wealth

Wealth protection is just as important as wealth creation. Without proper risk management, your financial achievements can be jeopardized by unforeseen events such as illness, economic downturns, or lawsuits.

Below is a breakdown of key strategies to safeguard your wealth:

1. Insurance: Essential Financial Protection

💡 **Purpose:** To protect yourself, your family, and your assets from financial loss due to unexpected events.

📌 **Key Types of Insurance:**

- **Health Insurance:** Covers medical expenses, easing the financial burden during health crises.
- **Life Insurance:** Provides financial security for dependents in the event of premature death.
- **Disability Insurance:** Replaces income if you're unable to work due to injury or illness.
- **Homeowners/Renters Insurance:** Protects against damage, theft, or liability claims.

- **Auto Insurance:** Covers vehicle-related accidents and associated liabilities.
- **Business Insurance:** Shields entrepreneurs from lawsuits, employee claims, or property loss.

✅ **Action Steps:**

- Review your policies regularly to ensure they match your current needs.
- Consider umbrella insurance for additional liability protection.
- Compare providers to find the best combination of premium rates and benefits.

2. Estate Planning: Protecting Your Legacy

💡 **Purpose:** Ensure your assets are distributed according to your wishes and avoid legal complications for your heirs.

◆ **Essential Estate Planning Tools:**

- **Will:** Clearly states how your assets should be distributed after death.
- **Trusts:** Help manage and transfer wealth while minimizing taxes and avoiding probate.
- **Power of Attorney (POA):** Appoints someone to handle financial or medical decisions if you become incapacitated.
- **Beneficiary Designations:** Ensure that retirement accounts, life insurance, and investments pass to the intended recipients.

✅ **Action Steps:**

- Work with an estate planning attorney to draft or update your will and establish any necessary trusts.
- Review and update beneficiary designations regularly to reflect life changes (e.g., marriage, divorce, children).

- Consider setting up a revocable living trust to streamline asset transfer and maintain privacy.

3. Diversification: Reducing Investment Risk

💡 **Purpose:** Spread investments across asset types to minimize potential losses from market volatility.

📌 **Diversification Strategies:**

- **Stocks & Bonds Mix:** Combine growth potential (stocks) with income stability (bonds).
- **Real Estate Investments:** Diversify through rental properties, REITs, or real estate funds.
- **Alternative Investments:** Include commodities, private equity, cryptocurrencies, or hedge funds.
- **Geographic Diversification:** Invest in global markets to reduce country-specific risks.
- **Business Revenue Streams:** Entrepreneurs should diversify products/services to stabilize income.

✅ **Action Steps:**

- Avoid relying too heavily on any single asset class.
- Use index funds or ETFs for built-in diversification.
- Rebalance your portfolio annually to maintain your desired risk level and adapt to financial goals.

4. Legal Protections: Safeguarding Personal Assets

💡 **Purpose:** Shield your personal wealth from legal disputes, creditors, and business liabilities.

📌 **Legal Strategies:**

- **Limited Liability Company (LLC):** Separates personal assets from business liabilities in case of lawsuits or debt.

- **Trusts:** Protect and manage assets, shielding them from legal claims or forced liquidation.
- **Prenuptial & Postnuptial Agreements:** Safeguard financial assets in the event of divorce.
- **Liability Insurance:** Covers legal fees and damages from lawsuits—especially important for business owners.
- **Asset Protection Structures:** Place assets in legally protected accounts or structures (e.g., offshore trusts in compliant jurisdictions).

✅ **Action Steps:**

- Consult an asset protection attorney to establish suitable legal safeguards.
- Keep personal and business finances separate (no mixed accounts).
- Use clear contracts and legal agreements to minimize potential disputes.

5. Tax Planning: Keeping More of Your Wealth

💡 **Purpose:** Minimize tax liability and maximize savings through smart planning.

📌 **Tax-Saving Strategies:**

- **Retirement Contributions:** Maximize 401(k), IRA, or Roth IRA limits to reduce taxable income.
- **Tax-Advantaged Accounts:** Use HSAs and 529 plans for tax-free savings on medical and education expenses.
- **Business Deductions:** Deduct eligible expenses like travel, equipment, and depreciation.
- **Tax-Loss Harvesting:** Offset capital gains by selling underperforming investments.

- **Estate Tax Reduction:** Reduce estate taxes by gifting assets or setting up family trusts.

✅ **Action Steps:**

- Work with a tax professional or CPA to optimize your strategy.
- Monitor tax law changes that affect your savings or investments.
- If applicable, consider relocating to a tax-friendly state for long-term savings.

6. Cybersecurity & Identity Protection

💡 **Purpose:** Prevent identity theft, financial fraud, and unauthorized access to sensitive accounts.

🔹 **Protection Strategies:**

- **Two-Factor Authentication (2FA):** Activate for all key financial, email, and investment accounts.
- **Credit Monitoring:** Use services like Experian, Equifax, or TransUnion to detect fraud early.
- **Strong Passwords:** Use unique, complex passwords and avoid reusing them across platforms.
- **Avoid Phishing Scams:** Never share sensitive data via email, links, or phone calls.
- **Freeze Credit if Needed:** Stop new lines of credit from being opened fraudulently in your name.

✅ **Action Steps:**

- Regularly update security settings on financial accounts.
- Consider identity theft insurance for added peace of mind.
- Store financial documents in secure locations (e.g., encrypted cloud or a locked safe).

7. Review & Update Financial Safeguards Regularly

💡 **Purpose:** Keep all protection strategies aligned with your evolving financial goals and life events.

📌 **Annual Financial Checkup:**

- **Review Insurance Coverage:** Adjust policies for life, health, auto, and property as needed.
- **Update Estate Documents:** Revise wills, trusts, and POAs after major life changes.
- **Rebalance Investments:** Ensure allocations match your current risk tolerance and time horizon.
- **Evaluate Legal Structures:** Confirm that LLCs, trusts, or asset protections still serve your goals.
- **Monitor Credit & Security:** Check for suspicious activity or unauthorized transactions.

✅ **Action Steps:**

- Schedule an annual financial review with a CPA, attorney, or financial advisor.
- Reassess protections after major life events (e.g., marriage, childbirth, inheritance).
- Stay informed on legal and financial updates that may affect your protection plan.

Final Thoughts: Building a Resilient Wealth Protection Plan

📌 **Wealth Protection Checklist:**

✅ Comprehensive Insurance Coverage (health, life, property, liability)

✅ Estate Plan in Place (will, trusts, power of attorney)

✅ Diversified Investment Portfolio (stocks, bonds, real estate, alternative assets)

✅ Legal Safeguards for Personal & Business Assets (LLCs, trusts, liability insurance)

✅ Proactive Tax Planning (retirement accounts, deductions, estate strategies)

✅ Cybersecurity Measures (password security, credit monitoring, fraud alerts)

✅ Annual Review & Adjustments (align with life changes and financial goals)

💡 ***The key to safeguarding wealth is preparation, diversification, and ongoing financial planning.***

3.5 The Role Of Financial Advisors

If managing your finances feels overwhelming, working with a financial advisor can provide clarity and structure. A qualified advisor can help you develop personalized investment strategies, optimize tax planning, and build a secure retirement roadmap.

1. Verify Credentials & Professional Certifications

💡 **Why It Matters:** Credentials ensure your advisor meets ethical standards and possesses the necessary financial expertise.

📌 **Key Certifications to Look For:**

- **CFP® (Certified Financial Planner):** Comprehensive planning, retirement, and wealth management.
- **CPA (Certified Public Accountant):** Specializes in tax planning, estate strategies, and business finances.
- **CFA (Chartered Financial Analyst):** Focused on investment analysis and portfolio management.
- **ChFC (Chartered Financial Consultant):** Similar to CFP but with a greater focus on insurance and estate planning.

- **RIA (Registered Investment Advisor):** Fiduciary advisors legally required to act in your best interest.

✅ **Action Steps:**

- Verify credentials through FINRA's BrokerCheck or the CFP Board.
- Ask about the advisor's educational background, experience, and areas of specialization.

2. Understand the Advisor's Fee Structure

💡 **Why It Matters:** Transparent fees help you avoid hidden costs and ensure advice is aligned with your best interests.

📌 **Common Fee Structures:**

Fee-Only Advisors:

- Charge a flat fee or percentage of assets under management (AUM).
- No commissions—ideal for unbiased guidance.
- Typical rates: 0.5%–1.5% AUM or $150–$400/hour.

Fee-Based Advisors:

- Charge fees and also earn commissions on financial products.
- May present some conflicts but often still provide full planning services.

Commission-Based Advisors:

- Earn primarily through the sale of investments, annuities, or insurance.
- Higher potential for biased recommendations.

✅ **Action Steps:**

- Ask directly: "Are you a fiduciary?" (Fiduciaries are legally bound to act in your best interest.)

- Request a written disclosure outlining all fees and potential commissions.

3. Assess Their Specialization & Expertise

💡 **Why It Matters:** Different advisors specialize in different areas of finance. Choosing one aligned with your unique needs ensures more relevant and effective guidance.

📌 **Types of Financial Advisors:**

- **Retirement & Estate Planning:** Assists with 401(k) rollovers, pensions, and trust management.
- **Investment Management:** Focuses on building and managing portfolios with stocks, bonds, ETFs, and alternatives.
- **Tax Strategy & Wealth Preservation:** Best suited for high-net-worth individuals, families, and business owners.
- **Debt Management & Budgeting:** Helps reduce debt and build long-term financial health through disciplined planning.

✅ **Action Steps:**

- Ask: ***"What types of clients do you typically serve?"***
- Select an advisor with proven experience in your specific financial situation (e.g., business owners, retirees, young professionals).

4. Check Reputation, Reviews & References

💡 **Why It Matters:** A strong reputation and positive client feedback are signs of trustworthiness and quality service.

📌 **Ways to Verify Credibility:**

- **Client References:** Ask for testimonials from past or current clients.
- **Online Reviews:** Check platforms like Google, Yelp, Better Business Bureau (BBB), and relevant financial forums.

- **Disciplinary Records:** Use tools like FINRA's BrokerCheck or the SEC's Investment Adviser Public Disclosure to verify background and check for complaints.
- **Industry Recognition:** Look for awards, speaking engagements, or articles that show thought leadership.

✅ **Action Steps:**

- Interview at least 2–3 advisors before making a final decision.
- Be alert for red flags: vague answers, fee avoidance, or pressure to commit.

5. Determine Their Communication & Accessibility

💡 **Why It Matters:** You need an advisor who communicates clearly, listens to your concerns, and is available when needed.

📌 **Key Considerations:**

- **Availability:** Do they offer quarterly, semi-annual, or as-needed check-ins?
- **Communication Style:** Are they clear, or do they overwhelm with jargon?
- **Tech & Transparency:** Do they provide online portfolio access, clear reporting, or mobile tools?
- **Personalization:** Are their recommendations tailored to your goals or overly generic?

✅ **Action Steps:**

- Ask: ***"How frequently do you meet with clients?"***
- Choose someone who is not only accessible but also educates you about your financial choices.

6. Confirm Fiduciary Responsibility & Ethical Standards

Why It Matters: Fiduciary advisors are legally obligated to act in your best interest—unlike some commission-based advisors who may prioritize product sales over your financial success.

How to Identify a Fiduciary Advisor:

- **Fee-Only Registered Investment Advisors (RIAs):** Must always act in your best interest.
- **Certified Financial Planners (CFPs):** Held to a fiduciary standard.
- **Avoid:** Brokers or commission-based advisors who may promote high-fee, non-essential financial products.

Action Steps:

- Ask: ***"Do you operate under the fiduciary standard at all times?"***
- Request a signed fiduciary agreement before making a commitment.

7. Test Their Investment Philosophy & Approach

Why It Matters: Advisors use different strategies to grow and protect wealth—choosing one that aligns with your values and risk tolerance is essential.

Investment Approaches:

- **Passive Investing:** Long-term, low-cost strategy using index funds and ETFs.
- **Active Investing:** Involves market timing and individual stock selection—higher risk, potential for higher returns.
- **Risk Alignment:** Portfolios should reflect your goals and risk comfort level.
- **Tax Efficiency:** Advisors should structure portfolios to minimize tax liabilities.

☑ **Action Steps:**

- Ask: ***"How do you select investments for your clients?"***
- Ensure their strategy matches your risk tolerance, time horizon, and financial goals.

8. Schedule a Free Consultation & Ask the Right Questions

💡 **Why It Matters:** A consultation is your opportunity to evaluate if the advisor understands your needs and offers the right approach.

📌 **Key Questions to Ask:**

- What is your investment philosophy?
- Are you a fiduciary, and how are you compensated?
- How will you help me achieve my financial goals?
- What happens if I choose to end our relationship?
- What sets you apart from other financial advisors?

☑ **Action Steps:**

- Prepare a list of your financial goals before the consultation.
- Compare responses from multiple advisors to make the most informed decision.

Final Thoughts: Choosing the Right Financial Advisor

📌 **Advisor Selection Checklist:**

☑ Verified Credentials (CFP, CFA, CPA, RIA)

☑ Transparent Fee Structure (fee-only preferred)

☑ Specialization in Your Financial Needs

☑ Strong Reputation & Positive Reviews

☑ Clear Communication & Accessibility

☑ Fiduciary Responsibility Confirmed

✅ Investment Philosophy Aligned with Your Goals

💡 **A great financial advisor will not just manage your money but also educate and empower you to make informed decisions.**

3.6 The Power Of Compounding

The Power of Compound Interest: **How Your Money Grows Over Time.**

Compound interest is one of the most powerful tools in wealth building. It allows your money to grow exponentially by reinvesting earnings—turning even small investments into substantial wealth over time. The key is to start early, stay invested, and let time do the work.

1. What is Compound Interest?

💡 **Definition:** Compound interest is interest earned on both the initial principal and the previously accumulated interest.

Unlike simple interest (which is calculated only on the original amount), compound interest accelerates growth the longer it's applied.

A= P(1+r/n)nt

Where:

A = Final amount after compounding

P = Initial principal (starting investment)

r = Annual interest rate (decimal form)

n = Number of times interest compounds per year

t = Number of years

✅ **Key Takeaway:** The more frequently interest compounds, the faster

your money grows.

2. Why Starting Early Matters

💡 The biggest advantage of compound interest is TIME. The earlier you start investing, the greater your returns—even with smaller contributions.

Example: Investing $10,000 at an 8% Annual Return

If you invest $10,000 at an annual return of 8%, and leave it untouched for 30 years, your investment grows dramatically:

Years Invested	**Balance (No Additional Deposits)**
10 Years	$21,589
20 Years	$46,610
30 Years	$100,627
40 Years	$217,245

📌 Key Takeaway: Your money more than doubles every 10 years due to compounding.

✅ The earlier you start, the less money you need to invest to achieve your financial goals!

3. The Cost of Waiting: A Real-Life Comparison

💡 Delaying investments reduces the exponential effect of compounding.

Example: Starting at 25 vs. 35 vs. 45

Assume you invest $200 per month with an 8% annual return, compounded annually.

Starting Age	Total Invested	Value at 65
25 Years Old	$96,000	$622,000
35 Years Old	$72,000	$284,000
45 Years Old	$48,000	$120,000

📌 **Key Takeaway:** Starting 10 years earlier can more than double your retirement savings.

✅ **Lesson:** Even small early investments outperform larger investments made later in life.

4. The Rule of 72: Quick Estimate of Doubling Time

💡 Want to know how long it takes for your money to double? Use the Rule of 72:

Years To Double: 72 / Expected Rate of Return

📌 ***Examples:***

- At an 8% return, money doubles in 9 years (72 ÷ 8 = 9).
- At a 6% return, money doubles in 12 years (72 ÷ 6 = 12).
- At a 12% return, money doubles in 6 years (72 ÷ 12 = 6).

✅ The higher the return, the faster your wealth grows.

5. How to Maximize Compound Interest

To take full advantage of compounding:

✅ Start Investing ASAP – Even small amounts will grow significantly over time.

✅ Reinvest Earnings – Let dividends, interest, and gains compound instead of cashing them out.

✅ Invest in Growth Assets – Stocks and index funds historically outperform inflation and fixed-income investments.

✅ Use Tax-Advantaged Accounts – 401(k), IRA, Roth IRA, and HSAs allow tax-free or tax-deferred growth.

✅ Make Regular Contributions – Consistency is key. Use dollar-cost averaging to reduce risk.

✅ Be Patient & Avoid Panic Selling – Let compounding work over decades.

6. The Snowball Effect: Small Contributions Add Up

💡 Even small monthly contributions grow significantly over time.

Example: Investing $100, $300, or $500 per Month at 8% Return

Monthly Contribution	10 Years	20 Years	30 Years	40 Years
$100	$17,300	$54,200	$149,000	$349,000
$300	$51,900	$162,000	$447,000	$1,048,000
$500	$86,500	$270,000	$745,000	$1,746,000

📌 **Key Takeaway:** Small, consistent investments lead to huge wealth over time.

✅ $300 per month can turn into $1 MILLION with enough time!

7. Common Mistakes to Avoid

● Starting Too Late – Waiting reduces your total gains.

● Not Reinvesting Dividends – This slows down compounding.

● Cashing Out Early – Selling too soon interrupts growth.

● Investing Too Conservatively – Low-interest accounts don't beat inflation.

✅ Long-term investing & patience are key to financial success.

Final Thoughts: The Power of Time & Patience

📌 **Key Takeaways:**

- Start investing as early as possible to maximize compounding.
- Even small investments grow into large sums over time.
- Use tax-advantaged accounts to keep more of your gains.
- Avoid panic-selling and let compounding work its magic.

💡 The best time to start investing was yesterday. The second-best time is today!

3.7 The Psychological Aspect Of Money Management 🌟

How Mindset Shapes Financial Decisions

Managing money wisely goes beyond crunching numbers—it requires discipline, awareness, and emotional control. Many financial decisions are influenced by psychological biases, upbringing, and societal norms. By recognizing these influences, you can develop better financial habits and avoid common money traps.

1. How Psychology Affects Financial Decisions

💡 Understanding your financial mindset is key to long-term success.

✦ **Common Psychological Factors That Shape Money Habits:**

✅ **Upbringing & Childhood Experiences:** Did you grow up in a household that prioritized saving or spending?

✅ **Emotional Spending:** Do you use shopping as a way to relieve stress or boost happiness?

✅ **Risk Aversion vs. Risk Tolerance:** Are you overly cautious or overly aggressive with investments?

✅ **Short-Term vs. Long-Term Thinking:** Do you focus on immediate gratification or future security?

✅ **Social Influence & Peer Pressure:** Are you trying to "keep up with the Joneses"?

✅ **Action Step:** Identify your money mindset (scarcity vs. abundance) and work on shifting toward long-term wealth-building behaviours.

2. Common Psychological Pitfalls & How to Avoid Them

● **Pitfall #1:** Lifestyle Inflation (The "More Money, More Spending" Trap)

💡 **What It Is:** As income increases, spending rises instead of saving the extra money.

✦ ***Example:*** A person who gets a $10,000 raise but spends it all on luxury items instead of investing it.

✅ **Solution:**

- Follow the 50/30/20 Rule (allocate 50% to needs, 30% to wants, and 20% to savings).
- Increase savings as income rises, not just spending.
- Set automatic transfers to savings and investment accounts before spending new income.

🔴 **Pitfall #2: Fear-Based Investing (Emotional Decision-Making)**

💡 **What It Is:** Making financial decisions based on fear rather than a sound strategy. (Added "a" for grammatical correctness.)

📌 **Examples:**

- Panic-selling during a stock market crash.
- Avoiding investing altogether due to fear of losses.
- Holding too much cash instead of investing for long-term growth.

✅ **Solution:**

- Follow a long-term investment plan instead of reacting emotionally.
- Use dollar-cost averaging (DCA) to smooth out market volatility.
- Diversify investments to reduce risk and build confidence.

🔴 **Pitfall #3: Overconfidence Bias (Thinking You're Smarter Than the Market)**

💡 **What It Is:** Believing personal skill alone determines investment success, while underestimating the risks involved.

📌 **Examples:**

- Taking excessive risks in day trading.
- Ignoring diversification because of past success with a few stocks.
- Assuming market downturns won't affect your investments.

✅ **Solution:**

- Avoid putting too much money into a single asset.
- Stick to evidence-based investing (index funds, diversified portfolios).
- Regularly rebalance your portfolio to avoid concentration risk.

Pitfall #4: The Instant Gratification Trap (Short-Term Thinking)

What It Is: Prioritizing immediate pleasures over long-term financial security.

Examples:

- Choosing a new car loan over saving for retirement.
- Spending bonuses instead of investing them.
- Using credit cards for unnecessary purchases.

Solution:

- Delay major purchases for at least 30 days to assess necessity.
- Automate savings to make investing effortless.
- Track expenses using budgeting apps to reduce impulse spending.

Pitfall #5: The "Keeping Up with the Joneses" Effect

What It Is: Feeling pressure to match others' spending habits, even if it's beyond your means.

Examples:

- Buying a luxury car because your friend did.
- Taking expensive vacations just to post on social media.
- Living paycheck to paycheck due to high-status purchases.

Solution:

- Focus on your own financial goals, not social expectations.
- Differentiate between wants vs. needs before making purchases.
- **Remember:** Wealth is what you don’t see (savings & investments, not luxury items).

3. How to Build a Wealth-Positive Mindset

✅ **Practice Mindful Spending** – Be intentional about how you use money. Ask: "Does this align with my goals?"

✅ **Set Clear Financial Goals** – Define specific short-term and long-term objectives (e.g., "Save $50,000 for a home in 5 years").

✅ **Create an Emergency Fund** – Having savings reduces financial stress and helps prevent fear-based decisions.

✅ **Learn the Basics of Investing** – Financial literacy empowers you to make informed choices.

✅ **Surround Yourself with Financially Smart People** – Your money habits are influenced by those around you.

4. The Power of Financial Discipline & Patience

💡 ***Wealth-building is a marathon, not a sprint.***

📌 **Smart Habits to Cultivate:**

✅ **Live Below Your Means** – Spend less than you earn and invest the difference.

✅ **Automate Your Savings & Investments** – Remove temptation by setting up automatic transfers.

✅ **Stick to a Long-Term Plan** – Market fluctuations are normal; stay focused on your growth strategy.

✅ **Embrace Delayed Gratification** – The biggest rewards come with time and patience.

💡 **Final Thought:**

Mastering money isn't about making the most—it's about managing it the best.

Chapter 4: Protecting Your Wealth

Wealth building is only part of the journey; protecting and sustaining it is equally crucial. Without a proper plan for managing financial risks, a lifetime of hard work and financial discipline can be undone by unexpected events such as economic downturns, health emergencies, or liability lawsuits. This chapter explores various strategies to safeguard wealth through risk management, insurance, and understanding market cycles.

4.1.1 Understanding Financial Risks

Types of Financial Risks and Their Impact:

- **Market Risk:** The possibility of investment losses due to economic downturns, inflation, or market crashes.
- **Credit Risk:** The risk of default on loans or credit obligations, affecting financial stability and creditworthiness.
- **Liquidity Risk:** The challenge of converting assets into cash quickly without incurring significant losses.
- **Inflation Risk:** The loss of purchasing power over time if wealth does not grow at a rate that outpaces inflation.
- **Legal and Liability Risk:** The financial burden arising from lawsuits, business liabilities, or regulatory penalties.
- **Health and Longevity Risk:** The financial strain caused by medical emergencies, disability, or outliving savings.

Risk Mitigation Strategies

1.Diversification: Spreading investments across different asset classes to reduce risk exposure.

Why Diversification is Important?:

- **Risk Reduction:** Different asset classes perform differently under various economic conditions. By spreading investments, you reduce the impact of any single asset's poor performance.
- **Stable Returns:** A well-diversified portfolio tends to experience smoother returns over time compared to an undiversified one.
- **Protection Against Market Volatility:** Market cycles fluctuate; diversification helps cushion against sudden downturns in any one sector.
- **Capital Preservation:** Reducing risk ensures that you don't lose a significant portion of your wealth in a single event.
- **Compounding Growth Opportunities:** Diversification allows you to benefit from multiple income sources, maximizing long-term financial growth.

2. Asset Allocation: Balancing risk and reward in your portfolio based on your financial goals, age, and risk tolerance.

Why Asset Allocation Matters?

- **Risk Management:** Different asset classes react differently to market conditions. A well-balanced portfolio reduces overall volatility.
- **Maximizing Returns:** The right allocation ensures that investors optimize gains while minimizing excessive risk.
- **Aligning with Goals:** Investors with different objectives (e.g., retirement, wealth preservation, or aggressive growth) require distinct allocation strategies.
- **Adapting to Life Stages:** Younger investors can afford to take more risk, while retirees need greater stability and income.

3. Emergency Funds: Keeping 6–12 months' worth of living expenses in a highly liquid account.

Why an Emergency Fund is Important?:

- **Financial Security:** An emergency fund ensures you can cover essential living expenses without relying on credit cards, loans, or other high-interest debt.
- **Peace of Mind:** Knowing you have a financial cushion reduces stress and allows you to focus on resolving the emergency rather than worrying about money.
- **Protection Against Life's Uncertainties:** Unexpected events like medical emergencies, car breakdowns, or sudden job loss can happen to anyone. An emergency fund helps you navigate these challenges without derailing your long-term financial goals.
- **Avoiding Debt:** Without an emergency fund, you may be forced to borrow money, which can lead to a cycle of debt and increasing interest payments.

4. Legal Protection:

Structuring businesses and assets to minimize liability exposure through LLCs, trusts, or other legal entities.

Why Legal Protection is Essential?

- **Prevents Personal Liability:** Proper legal structures separate personal and business assets, protecting individuals against lawsuits.
- **Minimizes Tax Liabilities:** Certain entities provide tax benefits and deductions that reduce overall tax burdens.
- **Ensures Business Continuity:** Legal structures safeguard businesses from legal disputes, ownership conflicts, and potential dissolution.
- **Protects Against Creditors:** Trusts and legal entities help shield assets from creditors and financial claims.
- **Facilitates Estate Planning:** Asset protection strategies ensure seamless wealth transfer to heirs and beneficiaries.

5. Hedging Strategies:

Using options, bonds, or commodities to counteract losses in high-risk investments.

Why Use Hedging Strategies?:

- **Risk Reduction:** Protects your portfolio from significant losses during market downturns.
- **Volatility Management:** Helps stabilize returns in unpredictable or highly volatile markets.
- **Preservation of Capital:** Ensures that your investment principal is safeguarded — especially important for retirees and conservative investors.
- **Flexibility:** Allows you to stay invested in high-risk, high-reward assets while limiting potential downside risk.

4.1.2 Risk Management and Insurance

The Role of Insurance in Wealth Protection:

Insurance acts as a financial safety net, ensuring that unforeseen circumstances do not erode your wealth. It is an essential component of a comprehensive financial plan.

Types of Insurance and Their Importance:

1. **Life Insurance:**
   - **Term Life Insurance:** Provides coverage for a fixed period, offering high coverage at a low cost. Ideal for income replacement
   - **Whole Life & Universal Life Insurance:** Offers lifetime coverage with a cash value component, sometimes used as an investment tool.
2. **Health Insurance:**
   - Protects against medical emergencies and hospitalization costs.

- Essential for avoiding financial setbacks due to unexpected medical expenses.

3. **Disability and Long-Term Care Insurance:**
    - **Disability Insurance:** Provides income if you are unable to work due to injury or illness.
    - **Long-Term Care Insurance:** Covers costs of assisted living, nursing homes, or in-home care, which can be significant in old age.
4. **Property and Liability Insurance:**
    - **Homeowners & Renters Insurance:** Covers damages to property and possessions.
    - **Auto Insurance:** Protects against financial loss from vehicle accidents or theft.
    - **Umbrella Liability Insurance:** Provides additional coverage beyond standard policies to protect against lawsuits.
5. **Business and Professional Insurance:**
    - **Business Interruption Insurance:** Covers lost income due to business disruptions such as natural disasters, fires, or other unexpected closures.
    - **Errors & Omissions Insurance (E&O):** Protects professionals against claims of negligence, mistakes, or failure to perform professional duties.

Choosing the Right Insurance Plan:

- Evaluate your needs based on financial responsibilities, dependents, and personal or business risk exposure.
- Compare policies based on premiums, coverage limits, deductibles, and exclusions.
- Ensure that chosen policies align with your long-term financial goals and overall wealth protection strategy.

4.1.3 Understanding Market Cycles

Market cycles refer to the natural fluctuations in the economy and financial markets, impacting investments, business profits, and overall wealth. Understanding these cycles can help investors and entrepreneurs make more informed financial decisions.

The Four Phases of the Market Cycle:

1. **Expansion (Boom Phase):**
    - Economic growth, rising employment, and increased consumer spending.
    - Stock market and real estate prices typically rise.
    - Interest rates are generally low, encouraging borrowing and investing.
2. **Peak (Overheating Phase):**
    - Maximum economic growth, but inflation concerns begin to arise.
    - Stock prices may become overvalued.
    - Central banks often raise interest rates to control inflation and prevent overheating.
3. **Contraction (Recession Phase):**
    - Economic slowdown, rising unemployment, and reduced consumer spending.
    - Stock markets decline, and real estate prices drop.
    - Credit availability tightens, affecting both business and consumer loans.
4. **Trough (Recovery Phase):**
    - The economy begins to stabilize and recover.
    - Stock prices bottom out, creating new investment opportunities.
    - Central banks may lower interest rates to stimulate economic growth.

Strategies to Navigate Market Cycles:

- **During Expansion:** Invest in growth stocks, real estate, and business expansion — but avoid excessive risk-taking.
- **At the Peak:** Consider reducing exposure to overvalued assets and securing profits. Diversify into safer investments to protect gains.
- **During Contraction:** Focus on capital preservation, increase liquidity, and consider defensive assets like bonds and dividend-paying stocks.
- **At the Trough:** Identify undervalued investments and begin reinvesting for long-term gains.

Avoiding Emotional Investing:

- Stick to a long-term financial plan instead of reacting impulsively to market fluctuations.
- Utilize dollar-cost averaging to invest consistently, regardless of market conditions.
- Maintain an emergency fund to avoid liquidating investments at a loss during downturns.

The Role of Debt in Wealth Building:

Debt is often viewed negatively, but when used strategically, it can be a powerful tool for wealth creation.

The key lies in understanding the difference between good debt and bad debt, and learning how to use leverage wisely.

This chapter explores how debt can either accelerate financial growth or become a burden that hinders wealth-building efforts.

4.2.1 Good Debt vs. Bad Debt ★

Debt itself is neither good nor bad — it depends on how it is used. Smart financial management involves leveraging debt to create value rather than being weighed down by liabilities.

What is Good Debt?

Good debt is money borrowed to invest in assets that appreciate in value, generate income, or contribute to personal or professional growth.

Properly managed, good debt can provide long-term financial benefits.

Examples of Good Debt:

Real Estate Investment Loans:

- Borrowing to purchase income-generating properties can create passive income and long-term appreciation.
- Rental income can cover loan payments while the property gains value over time.

Student Loans (When Used Wisely):

- Investing in education that increases earning potential can be a smart use of debt.
- Choosing cost-effective programs and pursuing high-return careers makes student loans more manageable and beneficial.

Business Loans:

- Entrepreneurs can use debt to fund or expand profitable businesses.
- If a business generates revenue that exceeds loan costs, the debt becomes a strategic tool for growth.

Low-Interest Home Mortgages:

- Owning a home can be a wealth-building asset if mortgage payments are sustainable and the property appreciates over time.
- Fixed-rate mortgages protect against interest rate fluctuations, making homeownership more predictable and financially stable.

Leveraged Investing (With Caution):

- Borrowing to invest in stocks or other financial assets can amplify returns, but it must be managed carefully to avoid excessive risk.

- Leverage should only be used with a clear risk management plan and a strong understanding of potential market volatility.

What is Bad Debt?

Bad debt is borrowing to finance liabilities or non-essential expenses that depreciate in value and do not generate income.

Accumulating bad debt can hinder financial growth and lead to long-term financial distress.

Examples of Bad Debt:

Credit Card Debt:

- High-interest credit card balances from unnecessary spending can quickly spiral out of control.
- Paying only the minimum amount significantly increases long-term interest payments.

Auto Loans (On Depreciating Vehicles):

- Financing expensive cars that lose value rapidly is a poor use of debt.
- Instead of buying new luxury cars, consider purchasing used or cost-effective options.

Personal Loans for Non-Essential Spending:

- Borrowing for vacations, gadgets, or luxury items can create financial strain.
- If the purchase doesn't provide long-term value, it's better to save up rather than borrow.

Payday Loans & High-Interest Borrowing:

- These predatory loans charge exorbitant interest rates, trapping borrowers in a cycle of debt.
- Avoid them unless it's an absolute emergency and there are no better alternatives.

4.2.2 Using Leverage Wisely

Leverage is the use of borrowed capital to increase the potential return on investment.

While leverage can accelerate wealth-building, improper use can lead to financial ruin.

Understanding when and how to leverage debt is critical to long-term financial success.

Principles of Smart Leverage:

- Leverage only for appreciating or income-generating assets.
- Ensure cash flow can comfortably cover debt obligations to avoid financial stress.
- Keep debt-to-income and debt-to-asset ratios within manageable and sustainable limits.
- Understand the risks associated with leverage, including market downturns and interest rate fluctuations.

How to Use Leverage Wisely in Wealth Building?

Real Estate Investing with Leverage:

- Investors use mortgages to buy rental properties, allowing them to own assets worth more than their initial capital.
- Rental income covers mortgage payments while the property appreciates over time.
- ***Example:*** A 20% down payment on a $300,000 property means the investor controls a large asset with a relatively small initial investment.

Stock Market Investing with Margin Accounts (High Risk!):

- Some investors use margin accounts to borrow money for stock purchases.

- If the stock price rises, returns are magnified — but if it drops, losses are also amplified.
- Margin trading is only recommended for experienced investors who fully understand market volatility and risk.

Business Expansion Using Debt:

- A well-structured business loan can help a company expand, increasing both revenue and profitability.
- Businesses should ensure that loan repayments remain affordable relative to cash flow.

Using Low-Interest Loans for Asset Growth:

- Taking out low-interest loans to invest in assets that generate higher returns can be a smart strategy.
- ***Example:*** If a business loan has an interest rate of 5%, but the business generates a 15% return, the leverage creates a positive financial outcome.

Mistakes to Avoid When Using Leverage:

❌ **Overleveraging:** Taking on too much debt relative to income or asset value increases financial risk.

❌ **Relying on Short-Term Market Fluctuations:** Borrowing to invest in assets that may decline in value leads to potential losses.

❌ **Ignoring Interest Rates:** Rising interest rates can make debt repayments significantly more expensive.

❌ **Not Having an Emergency Fund:** Without a safety net, unexpected financial challenges can quickly turn debt into a major liability.

❌ **Failing to Consider Worst-Case Scenarios:** Always evaluate what would happen if income drops or investments underperform.

Strategies for Debt Management:

Managing debt effectively is crucial for maintaining financial health and achieving long-term wealth-building goals.

Without a proper strategy, debt can become overwhelming and hinder financial progress.

This section explores proven debt repayment methods, strategies for refinancing and consolidating debt, and techniques for maintaining a strong credit score.

Debt Repayment Methods: Snowball vs. Avalanche

There are two popular strategies for paying off debt: the Snowball Method and the Avalanche Method.

Each has its advantages, and choosing the right one depends on your financial goals and psychological preferences.

1. The Snowball Method: Motivation-Driven Approach

The Snowball Method focuses on paying off debts from smallest to largest, regardless of interest rates.

The idea is to gain momentum by eliminating smaller debts quickly, creating a sense of accomplishment and motivation.

How It Works:

- List all debts from smallest to largest (ignore interest rates).
- Make minimum payments on all debts except the smallest.
- Put all extra money toward paying off the smallest debt first.
- Once the smallest debt is paid off, move to the next smallest, and repeat the process.

Example:

- $500 credit card debt (10% interest)
- $2,000 personal loan (15% interest)
- $5,000 auto loan (5% interest)

- $10,000 student loan (6% interest)

You would pay off the $500 debt first, then tackle the $2,000 loan, and so on.

✅ **Pros:**

- Provides quick psychological wins, keeping motivation high.
- Ideal for those who struggle with staying disciplined in debt repayment.

❌ **Cons**:

- Not the most cost-effective method, as higher-interest debts may linger longer.

2. The Avalanche Method: Interest-Optimized Approach

The Avalanche Method prioritizes paying off the highest-interest debt first, minimizing the total interest paid over time.

This method is mathematically the most efficient way to eliminate debt.

How It Works:

- List all debts from highest to lowest interest rate.
- Make minimum payments on all debts except the one with the highest interest.
- Put all extra money toward paying off the highest-interest debt first.
- Once that debt is paid off, move to the next highest-interest debt, and repeat the process.

Example:

- $5,000 credit card debt (22% interest)
- $10,000 personal loan (12% interest)
- $20,000 student loan (6% interest)
- $15,000 car loan (5% interest)

You would pay off the $5,000 credit card debt first because it has the highest interest rate, then tackle the $10,000 personal loan, and so forth.

✅ **Pros:**

- Saves the most money in interest payments over time.
- Faster overall debt payoff if discipline is maintained.

❌ **Cons:**

- Can feel slow in the beginning if high-interest debts are large.
- Some people may lose motivation due to a lack of early wins.

Refinancing and Consolidating Debt for Lower Interest Rates

Refinancing and debt consolidation can help borrowers reduce interest rates, lower monthly payments, and simplify debt repayment.

1. Refinancing Debt

Refinancing involves replacing an existing loan with a new loan that has better terms, such as a lower interest rate or an extended repayment period.

When Should You Consider Refinancing?

- If interest rates have dropped since you took out your original loan.
- If your credit score has improved, qualifying you for lower rates.
- If you want to switch from a variable-rate loan to a fixed-rate loan for more stability.
- If you need to reduce monthly payments by extending the loan term.

Common Types of Refinancing:

- **Mortgage Refinancing:** Replacing an old home loan with a new one at a lower rate.
- **Auto Loan Refinancing:** Getting a better interest rate on a car loan.
- **Student Loan Refinancing:** Consolidating federal and private student loans into one loan with improved terms.

- **Credit Card Balance Transfers:** Moving high-interest credit card debt to a card with a 0% introductory APR offer.

✅ **Pros:**

- Reduces interest costs and overall loan burden.
- Lowers monthly payments, freeing up cash flow.
- Can help accelerate debt payoff.

❌ **Cons:**

- May require a strong credit score for approval.
- Some refinancing options include fees or prepayment penalties.
- Extending the loan term can result in more interest paid over time.

2. Debt Consolidation: Simplifying Payments

Debt consolidation combines multiple debts into a single loan with a lower interest rate and a fixed monthly payment.

This simplifies debt repayment and can make managing finances easier.

Ways to Consolidate Debt:

- **Debt Consolidation Loan:** Taking out a personal loan to pay off multiple debts, leaving only one monthly payment.
- **Home Equity Loan or HELOC:** Using home equity to pay off high-interest debts.
- **Balance Transfer Credit Card:** Moving multiple credit card balances to a single card with a low or 0% introductory interest rate.

✅ **Pros:**

- Makes debt repayment more manageable with one consolidated payment.
- Often offers lower interest rates than standard credit cards.
- Can improve credit score by reducing credit utilization ratios.

❌ **Cons:**

- Requires good credit to qualify for the best rates.
- Balance transfer cards often have temporary low-interest periods (e.g., 12–18 months).
- Secured consolidation options (like HELOCs) put assets at risk if payments are not managed properly.

Credit Score Management: How to Maintain and Improve Your Credit

A good credit score is essential for securing low-interest loans, credit cards, mortgages, and even rental agreements.

Managing your credit score effectively ensures financial flexibility and better borrowing opportunities.

1. Understanding Your Credit Score

- A credit score (typically ranging from 300 to 850) is based on five key factors:
- **Payment History (35%):** Making on-time payments is the most significant factor.
- **Credit Utilization (30%):** Using less than 30% of your available credit boosts your score.
- **Credit Age (15%):** The longer you've had credit accounts, the better for your score.
- **Credit Mix (10%):** A diverse mix of credit cards, loans, and mortgages is beneficial.
- **New Credit Inquiries (10%):** Too many hard inquiries can temporarily lower your score.

2. Tips to Improve and Maintain a High Credit Score

Pay Bills on Time:

- Late or missed payments hurt your score significantly.

- Set up automatic payments or reminders to ensure consistency.

Lower Credit Utilization:

- Aim to use no more than 30% of your total credit limit.
- Pay down high balances before they are reported to credit bureaus.

Avoid Opening Too Many New Accounts at Once:

- Each hard inquiry slightly lowers your score.
- Space out applications for loans and credit cards to minimize impact.

Maintain Old Credit Accounts:

- Keeping old credit accounts open helps maintain a longer credit history.
- Even if you don't use them regularly, keeping them open can positively impact your score.

Dispute Credit Report Errors:

- Check your credit report regularly for mistakes or inaccuracies.
- Dispute any errors with the credit bureaus to have them corrected.

Use a Secured Credit Card (If Needed):

For those with poor or limited credit, secured credit cards can help rebuild credit by requiring a refundable deposit.

Diversify Your Credit Types:

Having a mix of revolving credit (credit cards) and instalment loans (such as mortgages or auto loans) can improve your credit score over time.

Chapter 5: Path to True Wealth

1. Introduction: Wealth Beyond Numbers

We live in a world obsessed with metrics.

Net worth. Salary. Follower count. Portfolio performance. Square footage. Car model. Title. Degrees.

But when you strip away the surface and stand in the stillness of your own life—

What do all those numbers really mean?

Can they hold you when you're grieving?

Can they heal a broken relationship?

Can they give you time with your aging parents, or laughter with your kids, or peace when you close your eyes at night?

Wealth is not a number. It's a state of being.

Let's get brutally honest: our culture equates financial success with life success.

We worship productivity, glorify hustle, and celebrate those who accumulate.

But behind many high earners, there's burnout, stress, and a quiet sense of emptiness.

Wealth, in its truest form, is much more internal than external.

It's about how free you feel, how calm your mind is, how deeply you love, and how fully you live.

If your bank account is full but your days are frantic, your relationships are strained, and your health is neglected—you are not wealthy.

You're merely surviving at a higher income bracket.

Rewriting the Narrative

Wealth beyond numbers asks:

- What's the point of earning more if you never have time to enjoy it?
- What's the use of a luxury home if you come back exhausted and disconnected?
- Why chase early retirement if you have no idea what you're retiring to?

Here's the truth: **Money is a vehicle, not a destination.**

Financial wealth is only one leg of the journey. It's a powerful enabler, yes — but it should serve you, not enslave you.

Too many people trap themselves in a life they built for others.

The house. The job. The car. The expectations.

All designed to impress, prove, or conform.

Meanwhile, their souls are starving — for meaning, freedom, and joy.

Real wealth is the ability to wake up on a Monday morning and choose.

Real wealth is having options.

Real wealth is being able to walk away — from a toxic boss, a draining contract, or a city that no longer inspires you.

Real wealth is peace of mind, energy in your body, laughter in your home, and clarity in your purpose.

The Misconception of "Making It"

We've been sold a lie:

That once we hit a certain income — once we "make it" — we'll finally be safe, happy, and fulfilled.

But here's what really happens:

- You make more, and your lifestyle expands.

- You buy nicer things, and suddenly you have to earn even more to maintain them.
- You reach one milestone, and another looms just ahead — always just out of reach.

The finish line keeps moving.

The goalposts are rigged.

And so you run — and run — and run.

But what if... you stopped running?

What if you redefined "making it" as waking up rested, spending the day doing what you love, surrounded by people who respect you —

and knowing your bills are paid — not because you earn millions, but because your life is aligned?

What if true wealth isn't in reaching, but in releasing?

Money is Neutral. Your Intentions Are Not.

Let's be clear: ***Money is not evil.***

It's not good either.

It's neutral.

It simply amplifies who you already are.

If you're generous, more money makes you philanthropic.

If you're insecure, more money makes you flashy.

If you're stressed, more money makes you anxious about keeping it.

Money doesn't solve emotional or spiritual poverty.

It can buy a vacation, but not inner peace.

It can build a house, but not a home.

It can fund a lifestyle, but not a life of purpose.

Which is why wealth without self-awareness is dangerous.

It leads to performative living, fragile egos, and shallow goals.

It leads to burnout disguised as ambition.

It leads to abundance that never feels like enough.

But wealth with intention?

That's transformational.

It allows you to live rooted in values, guided by purpose, and free from fear.

The Starting Point of True Wealth

So, what does this mean for you — right now?

It means your journey to true wealth doesn't start with your paycheck, your investments, or your career strategy.

It starts with one simple, radical question:

What does wealth mean to me — personally, deeply, honestly?

Maybe it's...

- Working four hours a day and spending the rest painting or hiking.
- Moving to a quieter place where your cost of living drops and your joy rises.
- Building generational wealth — and teaching your kids how to steward it wisely.
- Paying off your debt and never feeling that weight again.
- Retiring early so you can start a nonprofit or mentor young entrepreneurs.

There's no universal definition of wealth.

There's only your own — and your courage to build it intentionally.

So as we begin this final chapter, I invite you to let go of comparison.

Release the pressure to perform.

Stop measuring your success by someone else's scoreboard.

This is your wealth story now.

And it starts by looking inward before looking outward.

Because the richest life you can live is the one where money is the quiet engine — not the loud master.

2. The Four Dimensions of True Wealth

When most people think of wealth, they imagine dollar signs.

Investments. Luxury homes. Exotic vacations.

A specific number in a bank account that magically signals, "I've made it."

But the truth is, many people who look "wealthy" on paper feel empty inside.

Wealth without balance is like a table with one leg.

No matter how polished that leg is, the table will collapse under pressure.

That's because true wealth is multidimensional.

It's not just about how much money you have — it's about how whole your life feels.

To live truly wealthy, you must build across four core dimensions:

1. Financial Wealth — Security and Flexibility

Let's start with the most obvious dimension: **money.**

Financial wealth is the foundation.

It gives you stability, freedom, and the ability to make choices without fear.

It allows you to walk away from a toxic job, say yes to new opportunities, and sleep well at night knowing your future is secure.

But financial wealth isn't just about being "rich." It's about:

Having a safety net (emergency fund, insurance, passive income)

Being free from high-interest debt

Owning income-producing assets

Understanding how money works — so you're not manipulated by it

A person earning $60,000 a year with no debt, minimal expenses, and a joyful lifestyle could be far wealthier than someone making $300,000 a year, drowning in debt, and chained to a 70-hour workweek.

Example:

Tina, a freelance graphic designer, earns modestly but lives simply.

She has six months of emergency savings, works from home, and sets her own hours.

Her clients respect her.

She spends her afternoons gardening.

She's not flashy — but she's free.

That's **financial wealth with purpose.**

Financial wealth isn't about how much you make — it's about how well you use what you have.

2. Time Wealth — The Currency of Life

Time is the only currency you can never earn back.

It's non-renewable. Non-refundable.

And yet, most people trade time for money — only to later spend that money trying to reclaim time through convenience, technology, or early retirement.

Time wealth is about control over your schedule.

It's the ability to:

- Wake up without an alarm

- Say no to meetings that drain you
- Spend an afternoon with your kids
- Take a weekday off just because the weather's beautiful

If money buys options, time buys experience — and experiences are what make life feel rich.

Example:

Jorge left his six-figure job in the city to work part-time as a remote consultant.

His income dropped by 40%, but his happiness increased tenfold.

He takes long walks with his dog, reads every afternoon, and never misses a family dinner.

He's not chasing wealth anymore — he's living it.

Real wealth is owning your time.

Not renting it out to people who don't care about your peace.

3. Emotional Wealth — Inner Peace and Resilience

Emotional wealth is the peace of mind that money can't buy.

It's the ability to stay grounded during uncertainty, to feel grateful in the face of challenges, and to respond to life — not react to it.

When you're emotionally wealthy:

Your happiness isn't dictated by external circumstances.

You don't panic when the market drops or when your income fluctuates.

You don't make decisions out of fear or ego.

You cultivate self-awareness, emotional intelligence, and calm confidence.

You're not chasing validation — you know your value.

Example:

Lena is a business owner. When her startup hit a rough quarter, she didn't spiral.

She paused, assessed, and adjusted.

Why?

Because she practices mindfulness, journals regularly, and surrounds herself with a strong support system.

Her emotional wealth made her financially resilient.

You can have millions and still feel poor — if you don't have peace.

Emotional wealth means you're not a prisoner to stress, anxiety, or fear.

You have clarity in chaos.

4. Purposeful Wealth — Meaning, Legacy, and Contribution

This is the deepest layer of wealth — and the one most often ignored until it's too late.

Purposeful wealth is about living a life that matters.

It's about using your resources — time, money, energy, influence — for something bigger than yourself.

It's knowing that you're not just consuming — you're creating.

Not just surviving — you're serving.

This kind of wealth answers questions like:

- Why am I doing all this?
- Who am I helping?
- What will I leave behind?

Purposeful wealth shows up in:

- Mentoring others
- Building something that outlives you

- Supporting causes you care about
- Passing down wisdom, not just assets

Example:

Amar built a software company and sold it at 45.

Instead of retiring, he used his wealth to start a mentorship program for underprivileged youth in his community.

He doesn't just have money — he has meaning.

Purpose doesn't mean you have to start a non-profit or write a bestselling book.

It means aligning your life with your values — however that looks for you.

Because without purpose, even the most luxurious life can feel painfully empty.

Living a Fully Wealthy Life

You are truly wealthy when these four dimensions come into alignment:

- Your money gives you freedom.
- Your time reflects your values.
- Your emotions are steady and strong.
- Your life leaves a mark.

When even one of these is neglected, the entire structure starts to wobble.

A financially rich person with no time? **Not truly wealthy.**

An emotionally stable person constantly stressed by debt? **Not fully free.**

A retired millionaire with no sense of purpose? **Drifting, not living.**

But when you build across all four dimensions — intentionally, patiently, and with clarity —

you become unshakeable.

You stop comparing.

You stop rushing.

You start living.

3. Redefining Success: What Are You Really Working For?

When was the last time you asked yourself:

"What does success really mean to me?"

Not in theory.

Not in comparison.

But in the deepest, most honest way possible.

We grow up with borrowed definitions of success.

From childhood, we're fed a cultural script:

- Get good grades
- Go to college
- Get a "respectable" job
- Climb the ladder
- Buy a house
- Have a family
- Retire at 65
- Then, maybe, enjoy life

This linear blueprint becomes the unquestioned path.

And without realizing it, many people spend their lives chasing a version of success they never stopped to define for themselves.

But here's the truth:

If you don't define success for yourself, the world will define it for you — and it will sell you a version that keeps you busy, distracted, and unfulfilled.

Let's break that cycle.

The Danger of Default Success

Default success is the one-size-fits-all life model:

Earn more. Do more. Own more.

It's performance-driven.

It thrives on comparison.

It pressures you into milestones you didn't choose, timelines you didn't set, and expectations that aren't even your own.

And here's the wild part:

Many people achieve this version of success.

They get the title, the house, the salary — and they still feel deeply dissatisfied.

Why?

Because they climbed a ladder that was leaning against the wrong wall.

They were "successful" by every societal metric — yet felt completely disconnected from themselves.

The Shift to Personal Success

True wealth requires a shift from default success to designed success.

Design success is intentional.

It's based on your:

- Values
- Priorities
- Lifestyle preferences

- Energy rhythms
- Vision of a fulfilling life

It's not about impressing others.

It's about building a life that feels good on the inside — even if it looks modest on the outside.

Example:

Amrita left her career in corporate law to start a slow-living blog and live on a small farm.

People called her crazy.

Her income dropped significantly.

But her stress melted away.

Her days became peaceful.

She reconnected with her health, her relationships, her creativity.

By society's definition, she "downgraded."

But by her own definition, she stepped into success.

And that's what matters.

You Have to Know What You're Really After

Take a moment and ask yourself:

- Are you chasing wealth, or are you chasing what you think wealth will bring you?
- Are you building a life for your soul — or your social feed?
- Are your goals your own, or are they inherited from someone else's fears and dreams?

Often, people aren't chasing success.

They're chasing approval.

Or safety.

Or love.

Or revenge.

Or identity.

That's not inherently wrong.

But it's important to be honest about your **why** — because your why will shape your how.

It will shape the entire journey.

When you know what success means to you, your life becomes clear.

You stop wasting energy proving things to people who don't matter.

You start living on purpose.

How to Redefine Success for Yourself

Let's walk through a simple framework to design your own definition of success:

1. Define Your Core Values

What principles do you want to live by?

Examples: Freedom, creativity, integrity, family, service, adventure, simplicity.

When your life aligns with your values, it will feel rich — even if your income is modest.

2. Identify What Energizes You

What kind of activities make you feel alive, focused, and fulfilled?

What drains you, even if it pays well or earns praise?

Energy is the compass. Follow it.

3. Clarify the Lifestyle You Want

Forget about what sounds impressive.

What feels good?

- Do you want to live in a small town or a big city?
- Do you thrive in structure or in flow?
- Do you want to travel often or build deep roots?

Your definition of success should match your natural rhythm — not force you into burnout.

4. Set Meaningful Goals

Once your values and lifestyle vision are clear, create goals that support them —

goals that excite you, not just ones that inflate your ego.

5. Decide What You're Willing to Sacrifice

You can have anything — but not everything.

So ask yourself:

What am I willing to trade for what I want?

Time? Comfort? Approval?

Every meaningful life involves trade-offs.

The key is making them consciously.

Your Success Can — and Should — Evolve

Here's another important truth:

Your definition of success will change as you grow.

What felt successful at 25 may feel hollow at 40.

The goals you outgrow don't make you flaky — they make you human.

Give yourself permission to evolve.

To let go.

To pivot.

To rise.

The real failure isn't changing direction — it's refusing to move when your soul is begging you to.

The Most Successful People Are the Most Aligned

Some of the most "successful" people in history — Einstein, Oprah, Steve Jobs, Maya Angelou, Naval Ravikant — weren't just financially wealthy.

They were deeply in alignment with:

- Their unique path
- Their zone of genius
- Their purpose

That's why they stood out.

That's why their work rippled.

They weren't chasing someone else's version of success — they were living their own.

And you can too.

Reflection Questions to Redefine Success

To end this section, take a moment to reflect on these questions:

💡 What does a successful day look like for me?

💡 What parts of my current definition of success feel inherited, performative, or outdated?

💡 What would I pursue if I didn't care what anyone thought?

💡 What do I want more of — and what do I want less of?

💡 If I died a year from now, what would I regret not doing?

These answers will point you to your true definition of wealth.

When you redefine success around your values, your energy, your joy, and your vision, you step off the hamster wheel — and onto the path to true wealth.

Because the only version of success worth chasing...

is the one that feels like home.

4. Case Study: Sarah Thompson — From Debt to Freedom

At one point in her life, Sarah Thompson believed she was doing everything "right."

She had a college degree, a master's in education, a steady teaching job in the public school system, and a reputation for being smart, reliable, and hardworking.

But beneath the surface, she was quietly drowning.

The debt spiral.

Like many millennials, Sarah had taken out student loans to pursue her education.

She told herself it was an investment. And in a sense, it was.

But the numbers were staggering:

- $65,000 in student debt
- $9,000 in credit card debt
- A $6,000 auto loan
- Living paycheck to paycheck with nothing saved

She was 31, making $47,000 a year.

She had no emergency fund.

And worse, she felt ashamed — even though she had done nothing wrong.

Her stress showed up in small ways:

- She avoided checking her bank balance.
- She made minimum payments and hoped for the best.
- She felt anxious every time the topic of money came up in conversations.
- She said "yes" to social events she couldn't afford, just to maintain appearances.

"***I felt like I was wearing a mask***," she said.

"***I was a teacher — supposed to be a role model. But I was scared, exhausted, and hiding.***"

The Turning Point

Sarah's financial awakening didn't come from a big event.

It came from a quiet moment of clarity.

She was scrolling Instagram one evening when she stumbled upon a post that said:

"Debt is a thief of your future. Get mad. Get free."

It hit her. Hard.

She realized her debt wasn't just financial — it was emotional.

It was robbing her of her peace, her sleep, her ability to say yes to new opportunities.

She was, in her own words, "working for the past."

That night, she pulled out a notebook and wrote at the top of the page:

"My Plan to Get Free."

She didn't know exactly how she'd do it.

But she was done waiting.

She was ready to take her future back

The Strategy That Changed Her Life:

Sarah started with a brutally honest budget.

She looked at every single expense — rent, subscriptions, snacks, impulse Amazon orders — and made two lists:

- ***Need to live***
- ***Nice to have***

She cut the "nice to have" list in half.

She cancelled two subscriptions, started cooking at home, sold old clothes, and got real about her lifestyle.

Then she tackled the debt.

She chose the Avalanche Method:

- Focus all extra money on the highest-interest debt (her credit card)
- Make minimum payments on everything else
- Rinse and repeat

To increase her income, she took on part-time tutoring, started writing blog content on weekends, and even sold digital planners on Etsy.

Her monthly income grew by about **$800**.

She also started using a free budgeting app to track every dollar — and created a mantra:

"Every dollar is a vote for my future."

The Emotional Side of the Journey

Paying off debt wasn't just about math.

It was about mindset.

Sarah faced temptation constantly — friends going on weekend getaways, new clothes she wanted, moments of stress that made her want to "treat herself."

But she kept a journal.

Every time she wanted to give in, she wrote down why she started:

- "I want to know what it feels like to be free."
- "I want to live without fear."
- "I want to choose my life — not be owned by it."

She also created small milestones — celebrating every $5,000 paid off with a $20 treat:

a nice candle, a solo movie night.

Nothing extravagant — but deeply satisfying.

What Changed?

By year three, Sarah had:

- Paid off all her credit card debt
- Eliminated her car loan
- Built a $5,000 emergency fund
- Reduced her student loans by more than half
- Started investing 15% of her income into index funds

She was still teaching — but now with a different energy.

She felt empowered, not trapped.

Her net worth went from negative to positive.

But more than that — **her mindset transformed.**

"I realized I was never bad with money.

I was just uninformed.

Once I learned, I couldn't unlearn.

And once I took control, I felt powerful in every part of my life."

Where Is She Now?

Sarah is now 39.

She's debt-free.

She has a six-figure investment portfolio.

She continues to teach, but she also runs a financial wellness blog for educators.

She offers courses, coaching, and even hosts weekend workshops.

She's not a millionaire (yet).

But she doesn't need to be.

She's living her version of success:

- Work she loves
- Time freedom
- Financial security
- Emotional peace

A growing sense of purpose

"To me, true wealth is waking up every day without fear.

It's knowing I own my life.

And that I can help others own theirs, too."

Lessons from Sarah's Journey

Let's break down the key takeaways from Sarah's story:

- **Start Before You're Ready**

Sarah didn't wait to feel "confident" or "qualified."

She started where she was — with a notebook and a decision.

- **Track Every Dollar with Intention**

Awareness creates power.

When you know where your money goes, you take back control.

- **Side Income is Game-Changing**

Even an extra few hundred dollars a month can drastically speed up debt payoff and boost confidence.

- **Celebrate Progress**

Big goals feel manageable when broken into bite-sized wins.

- **Financial Freedom is Emotional**

Her greatest reward wasn't the zero balance — it was the lightness she felt inside.

You Don't Have to Be Perfect — Just Persistent

Sarah's story isn't about perfection.

She made mistakes. She had setbacks. She cried. She doubted.

But she kept going.

And that's what separates those who dream of freedom from those who create it:

Consistent action. Clear purpose. Radical ownership.

Are you ready to meet the next version of yourself?

Because just like Sarah, your path to true wealth doesn't begin with a raise, an inheritance, or a financial windfall.

It begins with a decision.

A commitment.

A moment of truth.

And that moment could be today.

5. The Freedom Formula: Time, Choice, and Peace

What's the point of wealth?

Seriously — ask yourself.

Why are you working so hard, saving, investing, or even reading this book?

It's probably not just to stare at a large number in your bank account.

It's not to win some imaginary race or climb a ladder with no top.

It's because — deep down — you're chasing **freedom**.

- Freedom to wake up when you want
- Freedom to say yes to what inspires you and no to what doesn't
- Freedom to spend time with your loved ones
- Freedom from financial anxiety
- Freedom to live life on your own terms

This is what I call the Freedom Formula.

It has three essential ingredients:

1. Time — The Most Precious Resource

"Time is more valuable than money. You can get more money, but you cannot get more time."

— ***Jim Rohn***

Time is the only resource you can't earn back.

Yet ironically, it's the first thing people sacrifice in pursuit of money.

We work 60-hour weeks.

We take on more projects.

We say yes to obligations that drain us.

Why?

Because we've been taught that time is less important than income.

That you should trade it, sell it, stretch it.

That you should always be busy.

But here's the truth:

You can always make more money.

You can never make more time.

Time freedom means:

- Taking a walk in the middle of the day because it's sunny
- Going on vacation without checking Slack or emails
- Spending your most productive hours on things that truly matter to you
- Not having to constantly rush, explain, or apologize for needing rest

Time wealth isn't about doing nothing.

It's about choosing everything.

2. Choice — The Ultimate Power

There is something deeply empowering about having the ability to choose.

Choice means you are not a victim of your circumstances.

It means you have options — and options are everything.

- Want to take a break from work? You can.
- Want to start a business? You can.
- Want to relocate to a quieter town or travel for a year? You can.
- Want to say no to a toxic client, job, or project? You can.

This doesn't mean your life will be without challenge or complexity.

But when you have agency, life stops feeling like a trap — and starts feeling like a canvas.

Wealth gives you the power of choice.

And that power allows you to build a life by design — not by default.

3. Peace — The True Goal

What do you really want from money?

Freedom? Sure.

Comfort? Of course.

Adventure? Probably.

But at the core, what most people want is **peace**.

Peace of mind that the bills are paid.

Peace of spirit that they're living in alignment.

Peace in their body because they're not chronically stressed.

Peace in their relationships because money isn't a source of conflict.

Peace isn't passive.

It's earned — through clarity, boundaries, self-discipline, and smart choices.

Example:

Meet Jenna, a freelance copywriter who earns half of what she made in corporate.

But she lives in a smaller town, works 25 hours a week, does yoga every morning, and eats dinner with her partner every night.

Her life is quietly abundant.

No stress. No drama. No financial chaos.

That's wealth.

Peace is the highest ROI of wealth.

If your money isn't buying you peace, it's not working hard enough.

What the Freedom Formula Looks Like in Real Life

Let's play out a few scenarios.

Scenario 1: Financially Rich but Freedom Poor

Nathan earns $250,000 a year at a consulting firm.

He has an impressive condo, drives a BMW, and vacations in the Maldives.

But he also:

- Works 70+ hours a week
- Is on-call 24/7
- Hasn't had a real conversation with his parents in months
- Can't sleep without pills
- Is constantly worried about his image and reputation

He's financially rich.

But he has:

- No time
- No choice (he's trapped in golden handcuffs)
- No peace

He is not **truly wealthy**.

Scenario 2: Moderate Income, Maximum Freedom

Now meet Leah.

- She earns $70,000 a year as a remote UX designer. She:
- Works 30 hours a week

- Lives in a mid-cost town
- Bikes instead of owning a car
- Has a solid emergency fund and simple investments
- Spends weekends hiking, reading, and volunteering
- She has time, choice, and peace.

She's living the **Freedom Formula**.

Designing Your Own Freedom Formula

You don't need to be rich to start designing freedom into your life.

Here's how:

Step 1: Audit Your Time

Where are your hours going?

Track a full week. **Be brutally honest.**

Then ask yourself:

- What do I want to do more of?
- What can I delegate, automate, or delete?
- What's draining me?

Time freedom starts with time awareness.

Step 2: Create Space for Choice

Start building optionality into your life:

- A buffer in your savings account
- Flexible income streams (freelance, remote work, consulting)
- Skills you can use anywhere
- A life with low fixed expenses

The more leverage you have, the more choices you gain.

Step 3: Build a Peace Plan

What would a peaceful life look like for you?

- Fewer hours?
- Simpler routines?
- More nature?
- Fewer notifications?
- Lower bills?

Start protecting your peace like it's a paycheck.

Because it is.

When You Have the Freedom Formula, You Stop Compromising

You stop saying yes when you mean no.

You stop overextending just to prove your worth.

You stop tolerating situations that make you sick or small.

Because now, you have **time, choice, and peace** — the holy trinity of true wealth.

You start living like the main character in your life.

You don't need permission.

You don't wait for "someday."

You build your freedom now.

6. Wealth and Mental Wellbeing: Emotional Wealth as the Foundation

What if you had all the money you ever dreamed of, but your mind was in chaos?

What if your business was thriving, but you couldn't sleep at night?

What if you could afford luxury, but couldn't feel joy, stillness, or connection?

This is the silent epidemic in today's world:

people who are financially successful but emotionally bankrupt.

They've accumulated assets, built brands, and checked every box — but inside, they're anxious, reactive, numbed out, or on the brink of burnout.

Because wealth without mental wellbeing isn't wealth — **it's a trap**.

What Is Emotional Wealth?

Emotional wealth is the stability, strength, and peace within your inner world.

It's your ability to:

- Process emotions in a healthy way
- Maintain perspective under stress
- Feel joy, calm, and satisfaction — not just chase the next goal
- Build strong relationships based on trust and presence
- Sleep peacefully knowing you're safe and in control

You can't see emotional wealth on a spreadsheet.

But you can feel it:

- In your body
- In your thoughts
- In your conversations
- In your habits and how you treat others

It's the internal experience that makes external wealth actually worth something.

The Myth of "I'll Be Happy When..."

One of the greatest lies we tell ourselves is:

"I'll feel better when I have more money."

Sure — money can eliminate certain problems:

- It can pay the bills
- Create stability
- Unlock new options

But it can't fix:

- Low self-worth
- Trauma
- Insecurity
- Perfectionism
- Comparison
- Chronic anxiety

Those are inner issues that require **emotional discipline**, not just financial discipline.

You don't heal through wealth.

You heal by going inward — and then you amplify your peace through wealth.

Why Emotional Wealth Matters for Long-Term Success

Here's something every high-performing individual eventually learns:

Your emotional capacity will either multiply or sabotage your financial capacity.

Here's how emotional instability can undermine your success:

- You overwork to prove your worth
- You make impulsive decisions when you're stressed

- You self-sabotage when things are going well
- You spend money emotionally instead of intentionally
- You ignore red flags in business partnerships
- You can't rest — even when you've "earned it"

On the flip side, emotional wealth creates:

- Clear boundaries
- Better judgment
- Resilience during downturns
- Healthier relationships with money, people, and yourself

Emotional wealth is the anchor.

It keeps you grounded when everything else is shifting.

Signs You're Building Emotional Wealth

You don't need to be a monk or meditate for three hours a day to be emotionally wealthy.

But you do need to be intentional.

Here are some powerful signs you're on the right track:

- You respond to challenges with curiosity, not panic
- You know how to regulate your nervous system (deep breathing, rest, breaks)
- You don't tie your self-worth to your net worth
- You can sit with discomfort without immediately trying to fix or escape it
- You forgive yourself and others quickly
- You speak to yourself with kindness, even when you're not "winning"

Tools to Build Emotional Wealth

1. Journaling for Clarity

Writing is a powerful tool for emotional processing.

Try this prompt:

"What am I afraid of right now, and what's the truth beneath that fear?"

You'll be amazed how quickly clarity returns when you give your emotions a voice.

2. Daily Check-Ins

Each day, ask yourself:

- How am I feeling — really?
- What do I need right now?
- Am I acting out of fear or alignment?

Awareness precedes change.

These micro-reflections recalibrate you.

3. Boundaries Are Emotional Currency

If you don't protect your time, energy, and focus, your emotions will always be on edge.

Boundaries are a form of self-respect — and a requirement for emotional wealth.

4. Letting Go of the Inner Critic

You are not your productivity.

You are not your bank balance.

You are not your mistakes.

Silence the voice that says, "I'm only valuable when I'm achieving."

Replace it with:

"I am worthy now, and growth is my path — not my proof."

Emotional Wealth in Relationships

How you relate to others is a direct reflection of how you relate to yourself.

When you are emotionally wealthy, your relationships shift:

- You stop trying to fix or control others
- You communicate with clarity instead of defensiveness
- You celebrate others' success without feeling diminished
- You stop tolerating relationships that rob your peace

True wealth is a dinner table full of people who love you — not what you earn.

Case in Point: The CEO Who Learned to Slow Down

Jason, a 43-year-old tech CEO, once told me:

"I have everything I ever wanted. A beautiful family, a successful company, the house, the lifestyle. But I feel like I'm dying inside."

He wasn't exaggerating.

He was sleeping four hours a night, snapping at his team, and feeling numb even during family vacations.

He thought he had a time management problem.

But what he really had was an emotional burnout problem.

So he made one radical decision: **a 30-day pause.**

He stepped back:

- Worked only four hours a day
- Saw a therapist
- Took daily walks with his kids
- Meditated for ten minutes each morning

By the end of those 30 days, he didn't just feel better — **he came back to life.**

His business survived.

His relationships deepened.

His creativity exploded.

"It wasn't a reset — it was a rebirth," he said.

Emotional Wealth Is the Core of True Wealth

Let's be honest:

What's the point of financial freedom if you're emotionally enslaved?

If you have the house but can't sleep?

The partner but no intimacy?

The time but no joy?

You didn't come this far just to perform wealth.

You came to **experience it — fully, peacefully, authentically.**

And that starts inside you.

7. Case Study: James Patel — Legacy Through Contribution

In the world of wealth, there are few stories as humbling — and as powerful — as that of James Patel, a self-made real estate entrepreneur who turned a modest beginning into a generational ripple of impact.

But what made James truly wealthy wasn't the size of his portfolio.

It was the size of his vision.

The Humble Beginnings

James arrived in the United States at the age of 22 with nothing more than:

- A work visa
- A single suitcase
- $280 in his pocket

He slept on the floor of a shared apartment and worked 16-hour shifts at a gas station just to afford rent and groceries.

His parents had sacrificed everything to get him a plane ticket and an education in a new land.

There was no safety net.

No family wealth.

Just grit, responsibility, and dreams.

But James had a plan.

He studied relentlessly — real estate books from thrift stores, YouTube videos about investing, personal finance blogs.

He worked night shifts and used every spare dollar to pay off debts and save for his first investment.

The First Property

At 26, James bought his first property — a run-down duplex in a working-class neighbourhood.

- He lived in one unit and rented out the other.
- He slowly renovated it himself on weekends.
- He studied zoning laws, learned negotiation, and reinvested every cent.

He wasn't flashy.

He wasn't fast.

But he was focused.

By 35, he owned 12 properties.

By 40, he owned over 60.

His portfolio was now generating consistent cash flow.

But more importantly, James had created something few immigrants or first-generation families ever get to enjoy:

Financial independence.

He no longer had to work for money.

His money worked for him.

The Shift: From Accumulation to Contribution

James had what most people chase: freedom, assets, time.

But something didn't sit right.

He found himself reflecting often on his roots — his parents' sacrifices, the other families he saw struggling in the same neighbourhood he once lived in.

"I realized that money without a mission feels hollow," he later shared. ***"I had enough. Now I want to build something that would matter beyond me."***

That's when James began the second phase of his wealth journey:

Legacy through contribution.

The Scholarship Fund

It started with a single act:

A $10,000 donation to his old community college to start a scholarship for first-generation college students pursuing STEM.

But James didn't want his name on a plaque.

He wanted **impact.**

So he did something few donors ever do — he met with the students.

He offered mentorship.

He taught them about credit, savings, and investing.

He created a system where every scholarship recipient received one-on-one coaching for an entire year.

Within three years, his fund had grown and impacted over 60 students — many of whom were now graduating debt-free and financially literate.

Some even became landlords and small business owners themselves.

The Affordable Housing Project

James knew what it felt like to be unable to afford decent housing.

So when a large abandoned building in his old neighborhood came up for sale, he didn't hesitate.

He partnered with a nonprofit and used part of his portfolio profits to transform the property into affordable units for single mothers and working-class families.

The building included:

- A free financial education center
- After-school tutoring for kids
- On-site childcare services
- An emergency fund and job board for tenants

It wasn't just a building.

It was a system for stability.

When asked why he didn't just sell or lease it for market value, James replied:

"Because that would have made me richer. This makes me wealthier."

Building the Family Trust

James didn't just want to give back to the community — he wanted to ensure his own family would thrive for generations.

He created a family trust to:

- Legally protect his assets from taxes and legal claims
- Ensure his children would be stewards of the wealth, not victims of it

- Provide income for aging parents and extended relatives
- Fund future business ventures and community projects

More importantly, he made it a condition that every family member who received trust benefits must:

- Complete a financial literacy program
- Volunteer at one charitable event each year

"I'm not passing down just wealth," he said. ***"I'm passing down wisdom and responsibility."***

The Emotional and Purposeful Wealth

James's life became a masterclass in the deeper dimensions of wealth:

- **Financial:** A self-sustaining portfolio of real estate and businesses
- **Time:** Freedom to choose how he spent every day
- **Emotional:** Peace, gratitude, and alignment with his values
- **Purposeful:** An ongoing legacy of education, housing, and hope

His days were filled with conversations, mentoring, strategic philanthropy, and time with his children.

He was no longer chasing money.

He was directing it — like an artist with a brush, painting his legacy with every decision.

Lessons from James Patel's Journey

1. Focus First on Financial Stability

You can't pour from an empty cup. James built his foundation first — slowly, steadily, intelligently. Then he expanded.

2. Find the Mission Within Your Money

Wealth without purpose eventually feels meaningless. Contribution creates depth. And depth creates joy.

3. Legacy Is a System, Not Just a Statement

A will is not a legacy. A trust with principles, education, and community engagement — that's legacy.

4. Stay Rooted in Your Story

James never forgot where he came from. His values didn't change — only his capacity to live them fully.

You Don't Need Millions to Create a Legacy

Let's be clear:

You don't have to be a real estate mogul to live like James Patel.

You can:

- Start a micro-scholarship fund with friends or coworkers
- Mentor someone from a background similar to yours
- Volunteer your time or skills
- Teach your kids about compound interest and giving
- Invest in causes that mirror your story

True wealth is not about scale — ***it's about intention.***

James Patel didn't just build wealth.

He built a life so rich in meaning that even long after he's gone, his presence will still be felt — in students, homes, families, and futures.

That's the kind of wealth worth building.

8. Giving Back: The Role of Philanthropy in a Wealthy Life

There comes a moment on the wealth journey when you realize:

- You've taken care of yourself.
- You're building for your family.

- You've gained freedom, time, and peace.

So... Now what?

That question doesn't mark the end of your journey.

It marks the beginning of a new one — the shift from personal accumulation to collective contribution.

Because at the heart of every truly wealthy life is this truth:

What you give holds more power than what you keep.

Redefining Philanthropy

When you hear the word "philanthropy," you might picture billionaires funding libraries or cutting checks at galas.

But at its core, philanthropy is much simpler than that.

Philanthropy means:

- Giving intentionally
- Giving consistently
- Giving in alignment with your values
- Giving without needing applause

You don't need a million dollars to make a difference.

You just need a sense of responsibility — and the courage to act.

Why Giving Makes You Truly Wealthy

Here's what most people don't realize:

Giving is not a subtraction. It's an expansion.

It's not about losing something — it's about multiplying your impact.

Let's break it down:

1. Giving Increases Emotional Wealth

Acts of giving boost your mood, reduce stress, and create a sense of connection.

Neuroscience shows that generosity activates the same pleasure centers in the brain as food and love.

People who give regularly — whether time, money, or skills — tend to report:

- Higher levels of happiness
- Stronger social bonds
- Greater life satisfaction

Giving makes you feel rich — not just look rich.

2. Giving Strengthens Purposeful Wealth

When your money serves something bigger than your bills or goals, it becomes a tool for meaning.

Giving brings your values to life.

It's easy to say, "I care about education" or "I believe in sustainability."

Giving is how you back that up.

3. Giving Builds Legacy

Your name doesn't need to be on a building to leave a legacy.

Every life you touch becomes a thread in your story.

Every small contribution creates ripple effects you may never even see — but they exist.

They matter.

Types of Giving: Beyond Just Writing Checks

There are infinite ways to give. Here are a few:

1. Time

Volunteering your time is one of the most valuable and intimate ways to give.

It shows up in:

- Mentoring a student
- Helping a nonprofit with your skillset
- Visiting elders or assisting with community projects

Time is irreplaceable. That's why giving it away is so powerful.

2. Money

Yes, donating cash matters.

Whether it's $10 or $10,000, money provides resources that others can leverage.

Pro tip: Automate your giving.

Just like investing, consistent contributions compound over time.

3. Knowledge

Teach what you know. Share what you've learned.

Host free workshops. Answer DMs. Write blogs.

Knowledge, once shared, becomes infinite in its impact.

4. Platform

If you have a voice, use it.

Whether you have 100 followers or 1 million, amplify causes that align with your beliefs.

You don't need to be famous to shine in the spotlight.

Aligning Your Giving With Your Values

You'll feel most fulfilled when your giving reflects who you are.

Here's how to get started:

- Identify your core values (e.g., equity, education, environment, empowerment).
- Choose a theme or group to support (e.g., single moms, at-risk youth, mental health, clean water).
- Decide how you want to give (volunteering, monthly donations, content, community events).
- Set a giving goal (5% of income, 1 day/month of service, mentoring 2 people/year).

The key? Make it sustainable.

The Energetics of Giving

This might sound spiritual — but stay with me.

Giving unclogs the flow of abundance.

When you hoard out of fear, you signal scarcity to your brain — and your behavior follows.

When you give with intention and joy, you reinforce abundance.

You tell your subconscious:

"I have enough to share. I trust there's more coming."

This mindset unlocks:

- More openness
- Better decisions
- Deeper trust in yourself and life
- Magnetic energy that attracts opportunity

Abundance begets abundance.

The 5% Rule: Giving Like the Wealthy

Many people wait until they're rich to start giving.

That's backward.

The wealthiest people in the world started giving when they had little — and increased it as they grew.

Adopt the 5% Rule:

- Allocate 5% of your income (or time or energy) to meaningful giving.
- Automate it monthly.
- Revisit your giving goals annually.

It's a small number. But over time, it creates a massive impact.

And you don't need to advertise it.

Quiet giving is often the most profound.

Real-Life Example: The Barber Who Changed a Neighbourhood

Marcus owns a small barbershop in a low-income neighbourhood.

Business was okay — not great, but steady.

One day, he decided to offer free back-to-school haircuts for kids whose parents couldn't afford it.

No big campaign. Just a simple poster on the window.

That single act:

- Brought in dozens of families.
- Inspired other barbers to join.
- Sparked a local charity to sponsor more events.
- Brought Marcus unexpected media attention and a flood of new clients.

But more than that, it gave him purpose.

He started offering mentorship, resume help, and free financial literacy workshops on Sundays.

The barbershop became **a community anchor.**

Marcus didn't just make money.

He made a difference.

That's wealth.

You Are a Steward, Not Just an Owner

Let this land:

"The goal is not to die with the most money. It's to die having used your wealth to unlock as much good as possible."

Money will outlive you. The question is:

- What will it be doing when you're gone?
- Will it be tied up in unused assets?
- Or will it be active in the world — healing, building, educating, uplifting?

That's your choice to make.

And you can start right now.

In Summary: Giving is a Wealth Strategy

It's not fluff.

It's not charity in the guilt-driven sense.

It's **strategic.**

It's **soulful.**

And it's **legacy-level powerful.**

Give because you're grateful.

Give because you're ready.

Give because you can.

And watch as your definition of wealth deepens in ways you never imagined.

9. Simplicity and Minimalism: The Underrated Wealth Strategy

In a culture obsessed with more — more money, more clothes, more apps, more commitments — the boldest thing you can do might be this:

Want less.

Not because you're settling.

Not because you've given up.

But because ***you've woken up.***

Welcome to the quiet power of simplicity — the ultimate wealth multiplier.

Minimalism Isn't About Deprivation — It's About Liberation

Let's get one thing clear:

Minimalism isn't about living with bare white walls and two pairs of socks.

That's a stereotype.

Minimalism is about intentionality.

It's about removing what's unnecessary so you can focus on what's essential.

It's about asking:

- "Does this add value to my life?"
- "Is this helping me live with more clarity, purpose, or peace?"
- "Am I consuming out of alignment — or in alignment?"

True wealth isn't the size of your closet.

It's how free you feel inside it.

Why Simplicity is a High-Level Wealth Move?

You might be wondering — how is minimalism a wealth strategy?

Let's break it down:

1. Simplicity Saves You Money

The less you buy, the less you spend.

But more importantly — the less you want, the richer you already are.

When you stop buying things to fill a void, your finances stabilize.

- Impulse disappears.
- Debt declines.
- Savings rise.
- Investing becomes possible.

Suddenly, you're not fighting for wealth — you're attracting it through clarity.

2. Simplicity Buys You Time

When your calendar is packed with obligations you don't care about, you're bankrupt in time wealth.

Minimalism teaches you to say no.

- No to the extra meeting.
- No to the fourth networking group.
- No to the toxic group chat.
- No to what doesn't serve your mission.

The result?

You reclaim your hours — and with them, your life.

3. Simplicity Creates Mental Space

Cluttered spaces often mirror cluttered minds.

When you simplify your surroundings, your thoughts slow down.

- Decisions become easier.
- Anxiety lessens.
- Focus sharpens.
- Creativity flourishes.

Minimalism isn't just external. It's deeply internal.

How Simplicity Shows Up in Real Wealth

Here are a few real-world examples of how wealthy people live simply on purpose:

- Warren Buffett still lives in the modest house he bought in 1958.
- Steve Jobs wore the same outfit every day to reduce decision fatigue.
- Many millionaires drive Toyotas and live in regular neighbourhoods—because they value freedom over flash.

Why?

Because after a certain point, more stuff doesn't add more joy.

Once your needs are met and your financial base is solid, every new thing becomes either:

- A tool
- A distraction
- Or a burden

Minimalists choose only the first.

Digital Minimalism: Decluttering Your Attention

Wealth today isn't just measured in money.

It's measured in attention.

Your attention is:

- Sold by apps

- Hunted by ads
- Monetized by algorithms

But it's yours to protect.

Digital minimalism means:

- Fewer apps
- Curated inputs (news, podcasts, content)
- No mindless scrolling
- No unnecessary notifications
- Time-blocked tech use

Try this:

- Unfollow anyone who makes you feel behind, not inspired.
- Turn off all but essential notifications.

Spend one day a week offline—fully.

The result?

A quieter mind. More focus. Real connection.

And that's the beginning of peace-based wealth.

Minimalism in Business and Work

Simplicity isn't just personal.

It's also a professional advantage.

High-performing entrepreneurs often run lean businesses:

- Small teams
- Automated systems
- Low overhead

- Clear brand identity

Why?

Because complexity kills momentum.

And clarity is a competitive edge.

The same applies to your career.

Ask yourself:

- What if I simplified how I work?
- What if I did fewer things, but better?
- What if I focused on my zone of genius and delegated the rest?

Less scattered effort = more focused success.

How to Begin Living with Less but Gaining More?

Minimalism isn't a switch — it's a gradual shift.

Here's how to start:

1. Declutter One Area

Pick one drawer. One folder. One part of your calendar.

Ask:

"Do I use this? Does this bring value?"

If not — donate, delete, or delegate.

2. Review Your Subscriptions

Streaming services. Apps. Software. Memberships.

Are you actually using them — or just letting them auto-renew?

Cancel what you don't need.

Free up energy and cash flow.

3. Create a 'Not-To-Do' List

What drains you?

What obligations, people, or patterns add stress but no value?

Write them down.

Then make a plan to phase them out, lovingly but firmly.

4. Practice the One-In, One-Out Rule

For every new thing you bring in (physical or digital), remove something old.

It keeps clutter at bay — and forces you to stay intentional.

Minimalism Isn't About What You Give Up—It's About What You Gain

You're not depriving yourself.

You're delivering yourself — from excess. From pressure. From noise.

What you gain:

- Focus
- Presence
- Time
- Peace
- Clarity
- Cash
- Sanity

You're not "missing out."

You're opting into a life that's deliberately rich in space.

And that's the kind of wealth no algorithm can sell you.

Final Word: Choose Fewer, Better Things

Your energy is finite.

Your time is limited.

Your life is sacred.

Don't spend it maintaining things you don't love—or chasing things you don't need.

Simplify. Refine. Choose consciously.

Because in the end, the wealthiest life is the one where nothing feels like clutter—

and everything feels like a clear, intentional choice.

10. Case Study: Mia & Daniel – Retired in Their 40s

Mia and Daniel Robinson were the definition of successful—at least from the outside.

They were both high earners in their early 30s, living in a sleek apartment in downtown Seattle.

Mia worked in corporate tech.

Daniel was an attorney at a respected firm.

Together, they earned over $300,000 a year.

They had:

- Designer clothes
- Weekly fine dining reservations
- Two luxury cars
- Frequent travel
- A fast, polished life

And yet, they were deeply unfulfilled.

"We were constantly tired, constantly working, and constantly wondering, 'Is this it?'"

— Mia recalls.

The Wake-Up Moment

One evening, Daniel came home late—again—after pulling a 12-hour day prepping for a case.

Mia had just returned from a stressful product launch.

They sat in silence at the kitchen island, eating takeout they were too exhausted to enjoy.

Daniel looked up and said:

"Do you realize we're living for weekends and dreading Mondays... and we're going to do this for another 30 years?"

That was the first time they allowed themselves to ask:

"What do we really want from our lives?"

The answer wasn't more money.

It was:

- Freedom
- Simplicity
- Peace
- Adventure
- Connection
- Purpose

That night, they started a new kind of financial plan—not one that led to more spending,

but one that led to early retirement.

Discovering FIRE: Financial Independence, Retire Early

Mia stumbled upon the FIRE movement—a community of people aggressively saving and investing to retire decades earlier than traditional timelines.

It wasn't about never working again.

It was about having the freedom to choose what kind of work, if any, they wanted to do.

They binged blogs and podcasts.

They ran the numbers.

They looked at each other and said:

"We can actually do this."

And so they did.

The Shift: From High Lifestyle to High Freedom

Phase 1: Simplify

- Sold one of their two cars
- Moved from a downtown luxury apartment to a charming duplex in a quieter neighbourhood
- Cut dining out from 5x/week to once every other week
- Cancelled unused subscriptions, gym memberships, and impulse shopping habits
- Meal prepped, packed lunches, and learned to cook at home
- Created "no-spend" weekends focused on hiking, reading, and low-cost fun

This wasn't about suffering.

It was about reclaiming control.

"We realized we were outsourcing joy to convenience and consumption," Mia said.

"Once we slowed down, we remembered how much we loved just being together."

Phase 2: Supercharge Savings

- Went from saving 10% of their income to saving 55%, eventually hitting 70%
- Maxed out their 401(k)s, IRAs, and HSAs
- Invested the rest in low-cost index funds
- Opened a brokerage account for additional long-term growth
- Created sinking funds for short-term goals like travel and home repairs
- Fully funded a 12-month emergency fund to reduce fear and risk

They lived by one simple rule for every purchase:

"Will this add to our freedom—or delay it?"

Phase 3: Build Passive Income

Mia and Daniel didn't want to rely on investments alone. They built extra income streams:

- Created an e-book on budgeting and sold it online.
- Started a FIRE blog documenting their journey (which generated ad and affiliate income).
- Daniel took on part-time legal consulting projects.
- Bought a small duplex and rented it out for steady monthly cash flow.

Nothing flashy.

Just steady, intentional moves—brick by brick.

Retirement at 42 and 44

After 9 years of focused effort, Mia and Daniel hit their freedom number:

- $1.7 million invested.
- $300,000 in real estate equity.
- $80,000 in liquid savings.

They left their full-time jobs.

But they didn't stop working altogether.

They redefined work as:

- Writing
- Volunteering with local environmental nonprofits
- Speaking at financial literacy events
- Mentoring younger couples on the same path

Now, they "work" about 10 hours a week and live off a combination of passive income, rental profits, and a 3.5% annual draw from their portfolio.

They travel slowly, staying in one place for months at a time.

They live at a pace that feels real, grounded, and spacious.

"We didn't retire to stop working," Daniel said. ***"We retired to start living."***

Lessons from Mia & Daniel's Journey

1. Income Means Nothing Without Intention

They were already earning plenty.

The transformation came when they got clear on what their money was for—not just how much they made.

2. Your Lifestyle Can Be Rewired

Downsizing isn't defeat—it's liberation.

When you spend less, you need less.

And when you need less, freedom comes faster.

3. Small Decisions Compound

Every meal cooked, every subscription canceled, every dollar invested—it all added up.

Consistency was more powerful than any one-time windfall.

4. Freedom Is the Best ROI

Early retirement gave them back their most valuable asset: time.

And with it, they created purpose, joy, and impact.

Your FIRE May Look Different—And That's Okay

Mia and Daniel's story is one version of freedom. Yours might look different—and it should.

Maybe you want to:

- Work part-time instead of fully retiring.
- Live abroad, homestead, or pursue a creative career.

Take mini-retirements every few years.

Or simply create breathing room in your budget so you can say "no" more often.

The key is simple:

Design your money to match your dream—not society's expectations.

And start now.

You don't need to be rich.

You don't need a six-figure income.

You need vision, discipline, and a willingness to live differently.

A New Kind of Retirement

Mia and Daniel didn't wait until 65 to start living.

They **redefined retirement** as the freedom to live fully—not an escape from work.

Their story isn't about frugality.

It's about **focus.**

It's not about sacrifice.

It's about **saying yes** to what matters most.

And that is the kind of wealth worth building.

11. Wealth as an Energy: Abundance, Attraction, and Alignment

We've talked about strategy. We've talked about systems. We've talked about discipline.

But there's another layer to wealth that most people ignore—or misunderstand entirely.

Wealth is not just logic. It's not just effort. It's also energy.

Think about it: Money is a representation of value. And value is generated by energy:

- The energy you bring to your work
- The energy you hold around your goals
- The energy you carry in how you think, speak, and act about wealth

And like any energy—money is either flowing toward you or away from you.

Let's explore how abundance, attraction, and alignment work together to create a wealth vibration that fuels every other part of your journey.

Understanding the Energy of Money

Money is more than math. It's a movement.

It flows toward:

- Clarity
- Confidence
- Creation
- Contribution

And it moves away from:

- Scarcity
- Fear
- Chaos
- Inconsistency

If you've ever felt "stuck" in your finances, even when you're doing all the "right" things—this might be why.

You don't have a strategy problem. You have an energy mismatch.

1. Abundance: The Foundation of Wealth Vibration

Abundance is the belief that there's more than enough:

- Enough money in the world
- Enough opportunity
- Enough time
- Enough value in you to create and receive more

It's not blind optimism—it's a deep trust in expansion.

People with abundant energy:

- Share resources generously
- Take bold action without panic
- Attract opportunities, collaborations, and ideas effortlessly
- Make decisions from faith, not fear

Whereas people in scarcity energy:

- Hoard money
- Undercharge
- Overthink everything
- Panic when things go off plan
- Self-sabotage the moment they experience growth

Abundance isn't about what you have—it's about how you see.

2. Attraction: Magnetizing Wealth Instead of Chasing It

There's a difference between pursuing money and attracting it.

Chasing money feels frantic, tight, exhausting.

It's often driven by proving, pleasing, or surviving.

Attracting money feels powerful, open, and intentional.

It comes from alignment, self-worth, and value exchange.

To become magnetic to wealth, you have to:

- Know your worth (without needing external proof)
- Make bold requests (pricing, opportunities, raises)
- Stay in motion (clarity + action + energy)
- Let go of desperation (because people feel that frequency)

This is why some people with fewer qualifications land dream jobs or high-paying clients.

It's not luck—it's energy.

They trust themselves.

And others do too.

Money flows where confidence grows.

3. Alignment: Your Inner Compass to Financial Flow

Here's where it gets really powerful: Alignment is when your inner world matches your outer actions.

In simple terms:

- You do work that feels meaningful to you
- You charge in a way that honours your value
- You invest in things that reflect your goals
- You spend in ways that support your lifestyle vision
- You aren't chasing goals you secretly resent

When you're out of alignment, you'll feel resistance: burnout, confusion, stuckness.

When you're in alignment, things flow faster and smoother—because your energy is clear, congruent, and focused.

Example:

You say you want financial freedom, but you take on work that drains you, spend money to impress people you don't even like, and ignore your budget.

That's misalignment. And money senses it.

Now imagine this instead:

- You do work that energizes you
- You create a spending plan that supports your dream life
- You decline what feels forced or off
- You trust the seasons of ebb and flow

That's wealth in motion—driven by alignment, not anxiety.

The Money Mirror: Your Relationship with Wealth Reflects Your Relationship with Self

Here's something wild:

The way you handle money often mirrors how you handle your own self-worth.

- **Undercharging** = undervaluing yourself
- **Overspending** = trying to fill an emotional gap
- **Avoiding your finances** = avoiding your own power
- **Impulsiveness** = emotional reactivity
- **Extreme saving** = fear of not being enough

So if you want to shift your financial reality, you must shift your identity.

You don't get wealthy by doing more—you get wealthy by becoming more:

More trusting.

More clear.

More focused.

More empowered.

Rituals to Raise Your Wealth Frequency

You don't need to meditate for 12 hours or recite mantras until your voice is hoarse. But you do need consistency.

Here are some powerful daily and weekly rituals:

1.Wealth Identity Check-In

Each morning, ask yourself:

"What would the wealthiest, calmest, clearest version of me do today?"

Then act accordingly.

2. Money Gratitude Journal

Each evening, write down:

- Three ways money supported you today
- One financial win (big or small)
- One money belief you're choosing to reinforce

3. Money Visualization (3 Minutes)

Close your eyes. Picture the lifestyle, environment, and energy of your financially free self.

Feel it in your body. Let it anchor you.

4. Clean One Financial Corner

Each week, take one small financial action:

- Organize receipts
- Review subscriptions
- Adjust your budget
- Increase a savings goal
- Check in with your investments

Action clears energetic fog. Clarity equals momentum.

Wealth Energy Isn't Woo. It's Real.

This isn't about magical thinking.

It's about **energetic alignment and behavioural congruence.**

You can have a brilliant budget, but if you operate from fear, you'll never feel safe.

You can have millions, but if you're constantly trying to prove something, it'll never feel like enough.

You can make money from strategy—but you **multiply it through energy.**

Money is a relationship. Treat it like one:

- Be clear

- Be present
- Be respectful
- Be open
- Be consistent

And watch how it begins to respond in kind.

Last Word: You Are the Frequency

You don't chase wealth.

You don't beg for abundance.

You become the version of you who naturally receives it.

Because when you're in alignment—spirit, strategy, and soul—

you don't have to force success.

You flow with it.

12. Building Generational Wealth the Right Way

If you're reading this, there's a good chance you're not just trying to get rich for yourself.

You're trying to change the trajectory of your family.

You're trying to break cycles.

You're trying to rewrite stories.

You're trying to build something that outlives you.

This is the heartbeat of **generational wealth.**

But here's the truth:

Building wealth for the next generation isn't just about passing down money.

It's about passing down:

- Mindset
- Knowledge
- Systems
- Character

Because if you leave money without wisdom, you're not leaving a gift—

You're leaving a ticking time bomb.

Why Generational Wealth Fails

Research shows:

- 70% of wealthy families lose their wealth by the second generation
- 90% lose it by the third

Why?

Because most families focus on transferring assets—but not understanding.

They leave:

- Trust funds with no trust
- Real estate with no real education
- Money with no meaning

The result?

The next generation inherits financial power without the emotional, intellectual, or spiritual maturity to handle it.

"Wealth unearned is often wealth unkempt."

The Right Way to Build Generational Wealth

Here's how to ensure your wealth becomes a gift, not a curse:

1. Build Transferable Assets

Don't just work for money. Build things that outlive your labor.

Examples:

- Rental properties with positive cash flow
- Dividend-paying stocks or index fund portfolios
- Intellectual property (books, courses, digital products)
- Scalable businesses with leadership succession plans
- Royalties, licensing deals, brand equity

Key Principle:

Leverage.

Your assets should continue working—even when you don't.

These assets become the engine of generational wealth.

But the next steps are what keep the engine running.

2. Teach Financial Literacy—Early and Often

This is non-negotiable.

If your kids don't understand:

- Compound interest
- The difference between assets and liabilities
- How to budget, save, and invest
- The emotional triggers around money

...then you're setting them up to spend and stress, not steward and succeed.

Start small:

- Involve them in budgeting groceries
- Show them how you pay bills or track expenses
- Open a custodial investment account

Discuss how your values guide financial decisions

Then go deeper:

- Read books together
- Let them "manage" part of a family giving fund
- Encourage side hustles and let them manage earnings

Financial knowledge is the most valuable inheritance you can give.

3. Create a Family Wealth Framework

Most families talk about money only when it's urgent or uncomfortable.

Change that.

Create a culture of clarity and consistency.

Build a Family Wealth Framework that includes:

- Your mission and values
- Your long-term vision (freedom, legacy, service?)
- Financial principles (e.g., no consumer debt, 20% saving, 10% giving)
- Decision-making systems (Who manages what? When do we invest?)
- A shared calendar of "wealth conversations" (monthly or quarterly check-ins)

Make wealth a shared story—not a secret or taboo topic.

4. Use Trusts, Wills, and Legal Tools—But Don't Rely on Them Alone

Yes, you need the proper legal structures:

- A clear will
- A living trust
- Power of attorney

- Healthcare directives
- A well-planned estate

But legal documents alone are not enough.

Your heirs also need:

- A roadmap
- An education
- A mentor
- A sense of why the wealth exists

"You don't just pass down wealth. You pass down the responsibility of wealth."

5. Introduce Philanthropy Into Your Legacy

The wealthiest families in the world stay grounded through giving.

Examples:

- The Rockefellers created charitable foundations
- The Gates family pledged to give away billions
- Oprah founded a leadership academy for girls in South Africa

You don't need billions. You just need a spirit of generosity.

Teach your children:

- How to evaluate causes and charities?
- Why giving isn't about guilt—it's about agency and impact?
- How money, when stewarded well, can change lives beyond theirs?

Idea:

Create a **Family Impact Fund**—each member allocates a portion of money annually to a cause of their choice.

This builds empathy, purpose, and a shared mission.

6. Focus on Identity, Not Just Instructions

The strongest legacy isn't built from rules.

It's built from identity.

Help your family see themselves as:

- Builders
- Leaders
- Stewards
- Investors
- Creators
- Givers

When someone sees themselves as a wealth builder, they make very different decisions compared to someone who simply inherits money.

Identity fuels resilience. Identity fuels self-trust. Identity fuels growth.

Help them build an identity they're proud of—one that doesn't just preserve wealth but multiplies it.

7. Legacy Is More Than Money—It's Memory

Lastly, remember:

Your story is part of your legacy.

Don't just pass down bank accounts and properties.

Pass down your voice. Your lessons. Your struggles. Your humanity.

Ways to do it:

- Share your journey openly
- Talk about your mistakes as much as your wins

- Be transparent about what wealth means to you
- Record your voice telling family stories
- Write a letter to future generations
- Create a short video diary for your grandchildren

Money can be replaced. Your lived experience cannot.

When your heirs know why you built what you built, they'll honor it—not squander it.

13. Case Study: David Lin – The Legacy Architect

When David Lin was 12 years old, he stood behind the counter of his parents' dry-cleaning shop, handing out receipts and folding shirts.

It was his summer job—and, unknowingly, the beginning of a financial education that would shape his future.

"My parents taught me hard work," he says. ***"But they didn't know how to grow money. They knew how to earn it, save it, stretch it—but not multiply it."***

David would later become the bridge between generations.

He didn't just inherit a business—he reimagined what legacy means.

The Inherited Hustle

David's parents were Taiwanese immigrants who came to the U.S. with nothing.

They opened their shop with borrowed money, endless hours, and unwavering sacrifice.

They:

- Never took vacations
- Rarely ate out

- Poured everything into the business so their son could have opportunities

And David **did** have more.

He earned a scholarship to study finance.

He landed a prestigious job on Wall Street.

He lived the "American Dream."

But after five years in investment banking, something gnawed at him:

He was burned out. Disconnected. Miserable.

"I realized I was working in a world that celebrated wealth but didn't respect where I came from," he said.

"And I missed building something real."

At 30 years old, David made a bold decision:

He came home to take over the family business.

Everyone thought he was crazy.

The Reinvention

David didn't just want to run a dry-cleaning business.

He wanted to reimagine it.

He started with small but intentional changes:

- Moved operations to a bigger space
- Introduced eco-friendly, chemical-free processes
- Created a pick-up and delivery model using a custom app
- Partnered with local hotels and luxury condos
- Rebranded as a premium service provider

Within three years, revenue tripled.

By year five, he had franchised to 11 locations across two states.

But David's real goal wasn't just scaling.

It was securing—ensuring that his family's hard work would last,

not for five more years, but for five more generations.

Building the Family Wealth System

David began documenting everything:

- Processes
- Profit margins
- Vendor relationships
- Tax strategies
- Roles and responsibilities

He created a full business manual—not just for himself, but for whoever would come next.

He also established:

- A family trust to protect assets
- An investment fund seeded with 20% of annual business profits
- A family mission statement cantered on integrity, stewardship, and service
- Monthly "legacy meetings" with his spouse and parents to review finances and goals

"We stopped running the business like a hustle and started treating it like a holding company," David said.

Passing on More Than Ownership

David had two young daughters.

And while they were years away from understanding EBITDA or equity, he didn't wait to start teaching them.

He taught them:

- How compound interest works (using jelly beans!)
- Why giving matters (by letting them pick a charity each month)
- The difference between working for money and having money work for you
- The importance of identity: "We're Lins—we build, we give, we grow."

His parenting rule was simple:

"If I want them to be responsible with wealth, I have to train their character—not just their calculator."

Creating Community Legacy, Too

David didn't stop with his own family.

He expanded his legacy outward by:

- Hosting free business workshops for first-generation entrepreneurs
- Hiring and mentoring at-risk youth from the community
- Offering paid internships to high school students from underserved schools
- Creating a scholarship fund named after his parents

Because true legacy isn't just about what you leave for your family—

It's about what you leave through your family.

Navigating Family Challenges

It wasn't all smooth sailing.

There were disagreements—especially with his parents, who didn't understand all his changes at first.

There were hard conversations about money, roles, and retirement.

But David led with empathy and patience.

"I realized that if I wanted to modernize our family wealth, I had to honor the foundation they laid—even if I was building a new house on top of it."

Eventually, his parents came to respect not just his results, but his vision.

They began to dream again—not just of survival, but of ***impact***.

The Result: A New Kind of Legacy

Today, the Lin family has:

- A multi-million-dollar business with national reach
- A fully funded education account for both daughters
- A trust-managed portfolio of real estate and equities
- A philanthropic arm that supports three community programs
- A documented succession plan for the next 25 years

But more importantly, they have:

- Family dinners full of laughter
- Clarity around roles and responsibilities
- Open conversations about money, goals, and dreams
- A shared sense of purpose

David didn't just preserve the family business.

He turned it into a wealthy vehicle, a school, and a legacy laboratory.

Lessons from David's Story

1. Legacy Starts with Leadership

You don't need to wait for someone to hand you power.

Step into it. Own your future. Lead—even when it's hard.

2. Modernize the Past—Don't Erase It

Your roots are your strength.

You can innovate while still honoring tradition.

3. Teach the Why, Not Just the How

Systems are great. Values are better.

Train identity and purpose alongside strategy.

4. Think in Decades, Not Days

David made decisions not for immediate gratification, but for future generations.

That mindset created **exponential outcomes.**

You Are the Legacy Now

If you're building something—a business, a brand, a portfolio, a body of work—remember:

It's not just for you.

It's for everyone who comes after you.

You don't have to be perfect.

You don't have to be a millionaire.

You just have to be intentional.

And when you are, you're not just making money.

You're making history.

14. Spiritual Wealth: Purpose, Identity, and Inner Abundance

What if you gained the world—but lost yourself?

What if you reached every goal, hit every number, and bought every luxury... but still felt disconnected, restless, or numb?

This is the unspoken truth of wealth creation:

You can be rich and still feel poor if your soul is starving.

That's why we must talk about spiritual wealth—the deepest layer of abundance.

It's the part that doesn't live in your wallet, bank, or portfolio.

It lives in your heart, your spirit, your alignment.

Because true wealth is not what you have.

It's who you become.

What Is Spiritual Wealth?

Spiritual wealth is the sense of:

- Meaning in your daily life
- Connection to something greater than yourself
- Fulfillment beyond the material
- Peace in your decisions
- Alignment between who you are and how you live

It doesn't require religion or rituals.

It requires awareness.

It asks:

- Do you know why you're here?
- Are you living your truth?
- Are you contributing something real to the world?
- Are you expanding, evolving, and deepening as a human being?

Spiritual wealth is the fuel that keeps financial wealth from becoming an empty shell.

Signs You're Spiritually Wealthy

You don't need a monastery or mountain retreat to be spiritually rich.

You just need ***depth***.

Here's what it looks like in real life:

- You feel guided, not just ambitious
- You measure success by your growth, not just your gains
- You trust life's timing—even when it's inconvenient
- You can sit in silence and feel content
- You give freely because you feel full internally
- You pursue mastery—not just money
- You live by values, not by validation

It's a quiet confidence.

A soft power.

A steady flame that doesn't flicker when the wind blows.

The Danger of Spiritual Poverty in a Wealthy World

There are countless people who are:

- Multi-millionaires with anxiety
- Influencers with no identity
- CEOs who feel nothing in their marriages
- Creators who've lost their creativity
- Healers who can't rest

Why?

Because they were built externally but never anchored internally.

They chased applause, not alignment.

They served ego, not essence.

They looked rich—but felt empty.

"If your inner world is bankrupt, no amount of outer wealth can save you."

Building Spiritual Wealth in a Practical World

This isn't about escaping the world.

It's about engaging with it fully—on your terms.

Here's how you build spiritual wealth, day by day:

1. Define Your Personal North Star

Your North Star is your internal compass—the set of values and truths you live by.

Ask yourself:

- What do I believe in?
- What do I stand for?
- What would I die defending?
- What does a well-lived life look like for me?

Write it down. Revisit it often.

When you know your North Star, you stop drifting—and start directing.

2. Integrate Meaning Into Your Money

Instead of chasing money, ask:

- What will this money make possible?
- How can I use wealth to express my soul?
- What kind of world do I want to build with this success?

Make your finances reflect your values, not just your goals.

Examples:

- Invest in companies that align with your ethics
- Fund causes that speak to your heart
- Build a business that heals or uplifts others
- Turn your life story into a platform that empowers

This is what makes wealth ***holy***.

3. Prioritize Stillness

In a noisy world, stillness is a spiritual superpower.

Make time to:

- Meditate
- Pray
- Breathe
- Reflect
- Journal

Walk without distractions

Listen to the silence beneath the stress

Stillness reconnects you to your truth—and reminds you that you are enough, even without performance.

4. Let Go of What No Longer Serves You

Spiritual wealth grows when you stop carrying what's not yours:

- Expectations that aren't aligned
- Shame that was never yours to hold
- Hustles that no longer inspire you
- Identities you've outgrown

Letting go creates space—for clarity, for alignment, for grace.

It allows you to trade pressure for presence.

5. Remember Who You Are Without the Labels

Strip away the titles, the roles, the bank balance, the clothes.

Who are you then?

That person—the one beneath the armor—is your greatest asset.

Your soul is your brand.

Your spirit is your security.

Your essence is your empire.

You don't need to find yourself.

You need to return to yourself.

Spiritual Wealth Is What Carries You Through the Fire

There will be moments when:

- Markets crash
- Businesses fail
- People betray you
- Health falters
- Doors close

What gets you through isn't your strategy.

It's your **spiritual foundation.**

Your belief.

Your resilience.

Your faith in your worth.

Because when everything outside of you shakes, you can still stand firm inside.

That's real wealth.

Legacy Isn't What You Leave Behind—It's Who You Are While You're Here

People may forget your achievements.

They'll never forget your:

- Presence
- Peace
- Integrity
- Energy

"Your spiritual wealth is the part of you that echoes long after you've left the room."

Final Reflection

Wealth is not just about how much you earn.

It's about how **deeply** you live.

How fully you show up.

How courageously you love.

How aligned your inner world is with the outer one you're building.

Spiritual wealth is what turns a good life into a great one—

and a rich life into a real one.

15. Designing a Wealthy Lifestyle: Systems, Habits, and Boundaries

True wealth is not an event.

It's not a lump sum.

It's not a one-time jackpot.

It's a rhythm.

A system.

A way of life.

To sustain wealth—financial, emotional, time, or spiritual—you must design a lifestyle that supports it.

This isn't about hustling harder.

It's about structuring your days, your environment, and your decisions in a way that consistently aligns with your values, energy, and vision.

You don't accidentally fall into a wealthy life.

You build it—on **purpose.**

Let's explore how.

1. Build Systems That Support Freedom

Systems are how freedom sustains itself.

You can have all the right intentions, but without structure, you'll always fall back into reaction mode.

That's when stress creeps in—and wealth begins to leak.

Financial Systems:-

- **Automated savings:** Pay yourself first—before your bills, before your spending.
- **Investment autopilot:** Set recurring transfers into your index funds, IRAs, or brokerage accounts.
- **Monthly wealth review:** Once a month, review your finances: budget, income, expenses, net worth.
- **Bill batching:** Pay bills once a week or twice a month—organized, not chaotic.

Mental Systems:-

- Morning routines that ground you
- Weekly goal setting
- Regular journaling to clear the mental noise

Systems for decision-making (e.g., "If it's not a hell yes, it's a no")

Systems reduce decision fatigue—a hidden killer of focus and fulfillment.

2. Cultivate Wealthy Habits

You become what you do repeatedly.

Not what you intend, promise, or wish.

"You don't rise to the level of your goals. You fall to the level of your systems." – James Clear

So, let's define some wealth-building habits that move the needle every day.

Daily Habits:

- **Track your spending:** 2 minutes a day. That's it.
- **Move your body:** Wealth without health is a dead investment.
- **Plan your day the night before:** Control your time before the world does.
- **Read 10 pages of a growth book:** Money-making is mindset-making.
- **Ask one reflection question:** "Did I live in alignment today?"

Weekly Habits:

- Review your budget
- Set 3 "needle-moving" goals for the week
- Do one thing to invest in relationships: a call, a letter, a coffee
- Audit your calendar—what stays, what goes, what drains you?

Wealthy people don't just have better tools. ***They have better rhythms.***

3. Set Boundaries That Protect Your Energy

Boundaries are the walls that protect the life you're building.

Without them, you'll spend all your energy defending your peace instead of living in it.

Financial Boundaries:

- No unnecessary spending during emotionally charged times
- No lending money you can't afford to lose
- Saying "no" to people who expect access to your finances without offering respect

Personal Boundaries:

- Uninterrupted work hours—no meetings before 10 a.m., or one "deep work" day per week
- Social boundaries—spending time only with people who uplift, not deplete
- Rest boundaries—respecting your own need to unplug, detach, and recharge

Time Boundaries:

- No overbooking
- Protecting your mornings for high-leverage thinking
- Setting a clear cutoff time for work—because wealthy people rest, too

A boundary is not a rejection.

It's a recognition—of what matters, and what doesn't.

4. Design Your Physical Environment for Wealth

Your space reflects your standards.

And your standards shape your energy.

Set up your physical world to make success easier and friction lower.

Examples:

- Keep a clean desk = clearer focus
- Organize your financial folders = fewer missed deadlines
- Prepare healthy snacks = better decision-making
- Keep reminders of your goals visible = daily motivation
- Reduce visual clutter = calmer mind

Your environment should remind you daily:

"This is who I am. This is what I'm creating."

5. Build a Circle That Supports Your Standards

You can't live a wealthy life in a poor environment—including the people around you.

Audit your circle:

- Who stretches you?
- Who grounds you?
- Who triggers old patterns of scarcity or fear?

You need:

- 1–2 mentors (virtual or real-life)
- 1–2 peers who are on the same path
- 1 accountability partner or mastermind group
- A partner or close friend who supports your vision

Proximity is power.

The energy of your circle becomes the frequency of your life.

6. Create a Weekly Wealth Ritual

Pick one hour each week to check in with your vision.

I call this your **Wealth Hour.**

During Wealth Hour, you can:

- Review your finances
- Journal about your wins and lessons
- Learn something new (a blog, book, or course)
- Plan your investments
- Dream a little bigger

This isn't about control—it's about **connection**.

You're not just managing money.

You're co-creating a life.

7. Live Your Calendar Like You Live Your Budget

Most people budget their money.

Few budget their time.

But time is your greatest currency.

If I looked at your calendar, would I see:

- Room for rest?
- Time to create, not just consume?
- Space for family, play, and recovery?
- Alignment with your values and goals?

If not—redesign it.

Your calendar is not just a to-do list.

It's a reflection of your true priorities.

You're Not Chasing a Dream. You're Engineering a Reality.

This is the part most people miss.

They treat wealth like a goal, not a lifestyle infrastructure.

But wealth isn't just the result of what you do—

It's the byproduct of how you live.

Every day. Every week. Every quarter.

Design a life that:

- Honors your time
- Protects your peace
- Multiplies your value
- Amplifies your joy
- Feeds your spirit
- And allows you to keep growing—without burning out

This is what it truly means to ***live richly.***

16. The Wealth Trap: When Rich Isn't Free

Most people dream of being rich.

But few ask:

"What if I reach the top... and still feel trapped?"

It happens more than you think.

You earn more.

You achieve more.

You upgrade your lifestyle.

And then one day, you look around and realize:

- Your calendar is booked from 7 a.m. to 9 p.m.
- You have no space to breathe, think, or rest
- You feel pressure to maintain a brand, a reputation, a standard
- You're working harder after success than before

You've built a beautiful prison—made of gold, but still a prison.

This is the ***wealth trap.***

How the Trap Happens

It doesn't happen all at once.

It sneaks up on you.

It starts with good intentions:

- You want to grow your income
- Build a better life
- Provide for your family
- Prove something to yourself (or others)

But slowly, subtly:

- You begin to tie your worth to your work
- You take on too much
- You ignore fatigue because "this is the season to grind"
- You say yes when you should say no
- You outsource joy to your accomplishments

Eventually, you're successful on paper—

but inside, you feel hollow, exhausted, disconnected.

You got rich.

But you lost your freedom.

Signs You've Fallen Into the Wealth Trap

- You're constantly busy but feel unfulfilled
- Your rest days feel guilty, not restorative
- You feel pressure to maintain your income—even if it's hurting you
- You've lost touch with hobbies, fun, or simple pleasures
- You find yourself saying, "Once I just get past this next thing..." again and again
- Your self-worth rises and falls with your productivity

Sound familiar?

You're not alone.

And you're not broken.

But it's time to step back—and ***reclaim your freedom.***

What Rich Without Freedom Looks Like

Let's look at a few profiles. Maybe you'll recognize pieces of yourself.

The Overachiever

- Works 70+ hours a week
- Successful business or high-paying job
- Constantly chasing the next big thing
- Can't remember the last time they felt truly rested
- Gets sick often, but pushes through

Trap: Work has become an identity. There's no exit strategy.

The Lifestyle Prisoner

- Lives in a big house, drives a luxury car
- Kids in private school, vacations in style
- Monthly overhead is massive
- Feels stuck in a high-pressure job to "keep up"
- No freedom to pivot, downshift, or dream again

Trap: Success turned into survival. Choices feel limited.

The Personal Brand Burnout

- Big online following
- Monetized expertise or story
- Feels like they have to be "on" all the time
- Afraid to pivot or speak freely
- Creativity has turned into content fatigue

Trap: Authenticity replaced by performance.

The Root Cause: Success Without Self-Definition

At the heart of the wealth trap is this:

You built your life around goals, not values.

You followed a model of success, but never paused to ask:

- Does this feel good to me?
- Am I becoming who I want to be?
- What does my version of freedom look like?

You built fast. You built well.

But now, it's time to build with intention.

Escaping the Wealth Trap: The Path Back to Freedom

Here's how to shift from being rich and restricted to rich and free:

1. Reconnect With Your "Why Now"

You've grown. Your life has changed.

So your old why may no longer apply?

Ask yourself:

- Why did I start this journey?
- What did I hope it would give me?
- Is it still giving me that—or am I just maintaining momentum?

It's okay to evolve. It's okay to pivot. It's okay to say:

"This was good for a season. But I want something different now."

2. Redefine Enough

If you don't define enough, you'll never feel it.

There will always be:

- Someone with more
- Another level to reach
- A reason to keep pushing

But the wealthiest people are those who say:

"This is enough. I am enough. I don't need to prove anything anymore."

Ask yourself:

- How much money do I actually need to live well?
- What does a full life look like—outside of hustle?
- What would it take to work less, not more?

Define your finish lines—or you'll burn out chasing mirages.

3. Protect Time, Energy, and Joy Like Assets

If money is wealth, then time is luxury, energy is currency, and joy is ROI.

Build your life around those.

Ask:

- What would it look like to work four hours less each week?
- What drains me—and how can I release it?
- What brings me joy—and how can I prioritize it again?

Wealth isn't just in your wallet.

It's in your Wednesday afternoons and your Sunday mornings.

4. Set Boundaries with Your Ambition

Your ambition is a gift—but uncontained, it will consume you.

You need:

- No-go zones in your calendar
- Clear criteria for saying "yes"
- A refusal to sacrifice health, peace, or relationships for performance

You don't owe the world your burnout.

5. Normalize the Pause

Stepping back is not the same as falling behind.

Take a sabbatical. A digital detox. A low-output season.

Give yourself space to:

- Reflect
- Heal
- Reimagine

- Rediscover your voice

The world can wait.

And when you return—you'll return wiser, lighter, freer.

Success is Not Freedom Until It's Sustainable

What good is wealth if it:

- Robs you of rest?
- Costs you your health?
- Damages your relationships?
- Forces you to become someone you're not?

Real wealth allows you to:

- Walk away when something no longer fits
- Choose peace over pressure
- Be deeply present with people you love
- Create—not just perform

This is your permission slip to slow down, scale back, and build a life that fits your soul.

Because rich isn't free—unless you choose to make it so.

17. Embracing the Slow Game: Patience as a Superpower

If you could master just one trait to build true, lasting wealth, it wouldn't be hustle.

It would be patience.

Because while hustle gets headlines...

Patience builds empires.

"The strongest force in wealth creation isn't talent or timing—it's time itself."

— Warren Buffett (who made over 95% of his wealth after age 60)

Wealth—real wealth—is a slow game.

It's not built in sprints.

It's not measured in months.

It's built in seasons. Cycles. Quiet consistency. Long-term vision.

Let's talk about how to make peace with the slow—and use it to your advantage.

Why the Fast Game Fails

Everyone wants fast:

- Fast followers
- Fast returns
- Fast results
- Fast freedom

But fast wealth often leads to:

- Fragile systems
- Shaky mindsets
- High risk, low resilience
- Burnout, comparison, and anxiety

People who win the "fast game" often:

- Get overwhelmed by sudden success
- Spend faster than they earn
- Make impulsive decisions

- Struggle to maintain what they've built

💡 ***"Getting rich quick" is rarely sustainable.***

But getting rich slowly? That's where mastery lives.

The Slow Game Is a Mindset Shift

It's not about laziness. It's about strategy and vision.

People who play the slow game understand:

- Compound interest is magic
- Small habits create massive results
- Delayed gratification equals long-term peace
- Wealth isn't just built—it's earned, one decision at a time

They don't chase dopamine.

They chase durability.

The 1% Rule: Small, Daily Wins

If you improve just 1% a day, you won't be 365% better by the end of the year...

You'll be over 3,700% better—thanks to compound growth.

The 1% Rule is simple:

- Save a little more
- Invest a little more
- Learn a little more
- Focus a little longer
- Say no a little faster
- Say yes a little braver

That's how you go far without burning out.

Case in Point: The 10-Year Overnight Success

Almost every "overnight success" you admire has one thing in common:

They've been quietly working for years.

You just didn't see:

- The late nights
- The rejections
- The pivots
- The boring consistency
- The sacrifices

When they finally blew up, it looked fast.

But it was really a slow climb done well.

Slow doesn't mean stagnant.

Slow means sustainable.

How to Embrace the Slow Game in Your Wealth Journey

Let's make this practical.

1. Invest with a Long Horizon

Stop trying to time the market.

Stop panicking at every dip.

Buy and hold. Stay consistent. Let time do the work.

"Time in the market beats timing the market."

Set it. Automate it. Forget it.

2. Measure in Years, Not Weeks

Wealth isn't measured by what happens this month—it's what happens over decades.

So:

- Instead of checking your portfolio every day, check it quarterly
- Instead of panicking when income dips, zoom out to your annual trends
- Instead of chasing hacks, build rituals

Play long.

The results will compound quietly—and then all at once.

3. Build in Seasons

There will be times for growth... and times for rest.

Times to push... and times to protect.

Design your life in seasons:

- Creation seasons
- Deep work seasons
- Rest and recovery seasons
- Reinvestment seasons
- Expansion seasons

The slow game respects your rhythm.

What You Gain When You Slow Down

You gain clarity.

You gain confidence.

You gain space to breathe.

And more importantly:

- You make fewer mistakes
- You feel less pressure

- You protect your peace
- You stay in love with the process

Fast moves can make noise.

But slow moves build foundations.

The Spiritual Power of Patience

Slowness isn't just tactical. It's spiritual.

It teaches you to:

- Trust the process
- Let go of control
- Detach from ego
- Cultivate presence
- Embrace gratitude for the moment you're in

There's power in not rushing.

Power in sitting with your goals, feeling into them, and letting them grow in layers—not leaps.

Think:

Oak tree, not weed.

Cathedral, not pop-up.

Legacy, not trend.

Slow is Smooth. Smooth is Fast.

This military principle applies perfectly to wealth.

When you go slow:

- You make better decisions
- You create better systems

- You catch red flags early
- You enjoy the journey more
- You build something you can actually keep

The world may race.

But you—you are calm. Focused. Free.

Because you're not here for a quick win.

You're here for a long, rich, joyful life.

Closing Reminder: The Slow Game Is the Smart Game

In the end:

- Fast success fades
- Loud success burns out
- Shallow success collapses

But slow, intentional, aligned wealth?

That's the kind of success that lasts a lifetime—and beyond.

So breathe.

You're not behind.

You're just early.

And early is exactly where the builders of empires start.

Final Reflections: Wealth Is What You Make It

Here we are.

At the end of the road—and the beginning of a new one.

You've walked through:

- The foundations of financial stability

- The architecture of generational wealth
- The hidden power of energy, emotion, and identity
- The slow, steady rhythm of sustainable success

Now it's time to sit still for a moment.

To let it all settle.

And to ask yourself:

What does wealth mean to me now?

Wealth Is Personal

There is no universal formula.

There is no one-size-fits-all plan.

There is only you—and the life you want to create.

For some, wealth means early retirement.

For others, it means traveling the world, building a quiet home in the mountains, or raising children in a safe, nurturing environment.

For some, it means freedom from debt.

For others, it means funding nonprofits, mentoring youth, or creating art.

There is no wrong answer—only an honest one.

If you remember nothing else from this book, remember this:

The richest version of your life is the one you chose, not the one you copied.

Wealth Is Not a Destination

So many people treat wealth like a finish line:

- "I'll feel safe when I have $100K saved."
- "I'll be happy when I make six figures."

- "I'll finally be at peace when I buy the house, launch the business, and get the raise."

And then they get there... and the finish line moves.

The truth?

Wealth isn't a finish line. It's a way of being.

It's found in:

- How you show up daily
- What you prioritize
- What you believe about yourself
- What you're willing to let go of

The moments you say "yes" to rest, love, truth, and alignment

Real wealth happens in ordinary moments:

- It's brushing your teeth without rushing.
- It's laughing during a walk with someone you love.
- It's logging off at 4 PM because your work is done and your soul needs a sunset.
- It's the deep exhale of a life that no longer requires performance.

Wealth Is a Feeling before it's a Fact

Some people are broke... but feel rich.

Some people are rich... but feel broke.

The difference isn't income. It's energy.

Wealth is the feeling of being full.

Not overwhelmed. Not frantic.

Not drowning in debt—or drowning in to-do lists.

Full.

Full of choices.

Full of time.

Full of peace.

Full of connection.

Full of vision.

That feeling is available to you right now—not "someday when you make more."

Start feeling rich now, and watch how your outer world rises to match it.

Wealth Is a Ripple

The way you live... echoes.

- When you pay off debt, you model possibility.
- When you teach your kids about money, you shape generations.
- When you speak openly about your journey, you give others courage.
- When you give, you inspire.
- When you build with integrity, you build impact.
- When you heal your scarcity, you heal your family line.

Wealth isn't about what you keep.

It's about what you touch.

You are not just a consumer.

You are a creator—of energy, culture, safety, and power.

Own that.

Wealth Is a Choice You Make Daily

Every day, you choose:

- What to spend
- What to save
- What to say yes to
- What to walk away from
- How you treat yourself
- What you believe you deserve

Those choices don't have to be dramatic.

They just need to be aligned.

Aligned with who you are.

Aligned with what you value.

Aligned with the life you're building.

When you choose in alignment, your path will always lead to wealth—because it leads to wholeness.

You Are the Asset

You are your most powerful investment.

More than your job.

More than your bank account.

More than your strategy.

You are the one who makes the calls, takes the risks, pivots, builds, rests, grows, and leads.

Your mindset is the foundation.

Your habits are the bricks.

Your self-worth is the roof that keeps it all safe.

Protect yourself.

Nurture yourself.

Believe in yourself.

You don't have to be perfect.

You just have to be present. Intentional. Courageous.

A Final Word: Your Wealth Story Starts Here

This book was never about formulas.

It was about **freedom**.

Freedom to define success.

Freedom to trust your pace.

Freedom to say:

"I choose my path—and I walk it boldly."

Whether you're just starting or already miles ahead, remember:

- You are already enough.
- You are already capable.
- You are already worthy of a life that feels rich in every way.

From here forward, you're not just chasing wealth.

You're embodying it.

One decision at a time.

One breath at a time.

One aligned step at a time.

This is your path to true wealth.

Walk it boldly.

Live it deeply.

Build it wisely.

Share it freely.

You're ready.

Author's Message: Walk Boldly into Your Wealth

Dear reader,

If you've made it this far, let me pause and say something simple—but true:

I see you.

I see the version of you who picked up this book not just for information—but for transformation.

The one who is tired of chasing someone else's version of success.

The one who wants more—not just in money, but in meaning.

The one who's ready to take ownership of your time, your energy, your value, and your future.

If that's you—know this:

You were always meant for true wealth.

Not the kind that's flaunted, performed, or hoarded.

Not the kind that leaves you drained, disconnected, or anxious.

But the kind that is:

- Deeply rooted
- Quietly confident
- Undeniably yours

The kind of wealth that lets you wake up unhurried.

That makes you feel proud, not pressured.

That feeds your spirit while growing your bank account.

That wealth is not reserved for the elite, the lucky, or the chosen few.

That wealth is for anyone who decides to live intentionally.

And you just did.

You made it through 18 chapters of truth, clarity, strategy, and soul.

You explored:

- What wealth really means
- How to build it, protect it, and sustain it
- How to design a life around peace, not pressure
- How to redefine success on your own terms
- How to build a legacy that echoes for generations
- And most importantly—how to come home to yourself

Let that sink in:

This is not just the end of a book.

This is the beginning of your next chapter.

Let This Be the Line in the Sand

From this day forward...

- You don't just **make money**—you make decisions rooted in alignment.
- You don't just **save**—you build systems that support the lifestyle you love.
- You don't just **grind**—you act from a place of clarity, not compulsion.

You don't wait for permission.

You don't apologize for your dreams.

You don't dilute your vision.

You walk boldly,Strategically,

Freely.

Because the richest life you can live is one where:

- You know what matters.
- You say no with confidence.
- You say yes with joy.
- You're building, not just reacting.
- You're alive—not just functioning.

That's what I want for you.

And I believe, with everything in me, that you're ready for it.

If I Could Leave You With Just a Few Reminders...

Start where you are.

You don't need more credentials, more approval, or more luck.

You need action.

One step, right now, right here.

Define your own "rich."

Don't let society, social media, or your past define what your life should look like.

You have the right to design it your way.

Protect your peace like a paycheck.

Guard your energy.

Audit your circle.

Choose calm over chaos.

Walk away from anything that costs more than it gives.

Wealth is built in layers.

Financial wealth.

Emotional wealth.

Time wealth.

Spiritual wealth.

Build all of it—not just the part that fits on a spreadsheet.

💡 **Keep going.**

You'll stumble.

You'll doubt.

You'll have seasons where it feels like nothing's working.

But stay consistent.

Trust the compound effect.

Your future self is cheering for you.

This Isn't Goodbye—It's a Hand-Off

I've poured everything I know into these pages.

But now, it's your turn.

- To build.
- To lead.
- To rise.
- To create a life that's rich in every way.

You don't need to know the entire path.

You just need to keep walking—with ***clarity in your mind, courage in your heart, and purpose in your hands.***

And if ever you feel lost, stuck, or uncertain...

Just pause.

Breathe.

Remember this:

You are not behind.

You are not too late.

You are not too much.

You are exactly where you're meant to be—on the edge of a life worth living, a legacy worth building, and a wealth that can never be taken from you.

You got this.

With respect and belief in your journey,

—Vishal Uppal

Trilogy continues with Vol.2

Breaking all Myths

[*What Rich people do different than poor people?*]

www.ingramcontent.com/pod-product-compliance
Lightning Source LLC
LaVergne TN
LVHW052312200926
848481LV00002B/540
* 9 7 9 8 2 9 5 4 4 0 1 9 9 *